C000007145

Contents

Ex-LMS Class 5XP Jubilee 4-6-0 locomotive No. 45651 *Shovell* in Leeds railway station with the Thames–Clyde Express on 8 October 1951. The locomotive is displaying shed code 20A, Leeds Holbeck. The Thames–Clyde Express was a named express passenger train operating on the Midland Main Line, Settle–Carlisle Railway and the Glasgow South Western Line between London St Pancras and Glasgow St Enoch. Built at Crewe works in January 1935, No. 45651 remained in service until November 1962, when it was withdrawn from 84G, Shrewsbury shed, to be scrapped in December 1962 at Crewe Works. (YP. 6/C594)

Before closure of the Harrogate–Northallerton line, it was normal for some trains to be routed via Ripon instead of York. Here a Liverpool–Newcastle train draws into Harrogate, double-headed by Class D49/2 4-4-0 locomotive No. 62753 *The Belvoir* and Class B1 4-6-0 locomotive No. 61069. The line north of Harrogate was officially closed in 1967, though a limited number of freight trains used the line to Ripon until 1969. It was supposed that closing this stretch of line would have little impact, since passengers travelling north could join the East Coast Main Line at York. The stretch was temporarily re-opened as an emergency diversionary route during the Thirsk rail crash. The closure of the northern section of the line meant an end to over 100 years of railway service to the city of Ripon.

Introduction

My first book, *Doncaster Steam*, published in 1982, was an attempt to emulate five books titled *Yorkshire Steam – A look at Railways in the Ridings*, which were produced by the *Yorkshire Post* and appeared throughout the 1970s. Many of the pictures were incredibly sharp, full of incidental detail and captured the flavour of railways, mainly in the 1950s, which became the Indian summer of steam. I'm told the books quickly sold out and have been sought-after ever since.

I have been writing for the *Doncaster Star* since 1986 and recently this paper, along with what might be termed its mother ship, the *Sheffield Star*, was brought together with the *Yorkshire Post* under the Johnston Publishing umbrella. Through the deputy editor of the Sheffield Star, Paul License, I made contact with Peter Charlton, the editor of the *Yorkshire Post*, himself a former editor of the *Sheffield Star*. Knowing of the vast archives held at the *Yorkshire Post*, particularly the glass plates which formed the basis of the five *Yorkshire Steam* publications, I was able to put forward the idea of this present publication, *Yorkshire People and Railways*, and have it accepted.

Naturally, I wanted a chapter to include a selection of the pictures that were included in the previous five publications and which are virtually unknown to present-day steam enthusiasts. I have included ones which are most evocative of the times and give a real taste of what it was like to be part of the steam railway scene in the '50s. To me it is a dream come true to have my name associated with these pictures and I am sure people will share my enthusiasm for giving them a second airing. In most cases, I have greatly expanded the original captions to give full details of the locomotives and their association with Yorkshire, as well as any whimsical detail that is appropriate.

The other chapters deal with: Rail Crashes; Staff; Stations, Signal Boxes, Tunnels and Viaducts; Railway Heritage Centres; Naming Ceremonies and Other Events; and On Shed and Works. To compile these, I have looked through thousands of pictures and selected the 230 or so included here from a batch of around 1,000.

Throughout the Lineside section there is almost a continual mention of the locomotives built by the Doncaster Plant Works, a real birthplace for so many magnificent steam locomotives in the past, including the A1s, A4s and P2s.

If there is a chapter I like best, apart from the Lineside one, it is the Railway Heritage Centres section. In this, we see the county's early connection with railways at the Middleton Railway Trust, and if we then trip across to the North Yorkshire Moor's Railway, we quickly learn that the organisation is right at the forefront of running live steam excursions. *Tornado*, the first steam loco to be built in years, is trundling through the North Yorkshire countryside, along with other great steam locomotives. The other organisations, mainly run by armies of volunteers, at the Keighley & Worth Valley, Embsay & Bolton Abbey Steam Railway and the Elsecar Heritage Railway are all doing a great job and long may they continue to give future generations a real taste of the golden age of steam.

The Staff section is quite enlightening, not least for the involvement of women in an industry long considered a male stronghold. We see women as station announcers, swing-bridge operators, cleaners and as stewardesses. Long may their involvement continue.

The Stations section is tinged with sadness, as quite a number of the buildings have disappeared or been altered beyond recognition. Thankfully, however, some have been put to more imaginative uses.

Research for the book has mainly been carried out using the amazing newspaper archives on site at the *Yorkshire Post*, and I have been given much help by members of the photographic department, including Keith Hampshire and David Clay. My coordinator for the entire project has been the *Yorkshire Post*'s Paul Bolton. He has made pertinent suggestions about the book's content to make it a viable product in the already crowded world of nostalgia publications, particularly featuring railways.

I hope the reader has as much pleasure in looking at the book as I have compiling it because Yorkshire and its people have certainly made a contribution to the country's railway system.

Peter Tuffrey
May, 2011

One

Lineside

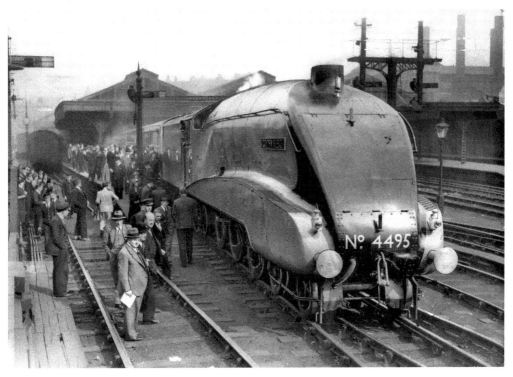

Leeds Central station with Class A4 4-6-2 locomotive No. 4495 *Golden Fleece* and the West Riding train set; the photograph appeared in the *Leeds Mercury* on 24 September 1937. Part of the caption beneath the picture read: 'The new LNER streamlined train [is pictured] before a demonstration run.' Each set of the West Riding Limited carriages consisted of eight vehicles, articulated in pairs, and they operated on the King's Cross–Leeds and Bradford service. The carriages were almost identical in design to those produced for the 'Coronation' sets, differing only in their internal colour schemes. When built at Doncaster in August 1937, No. 4495 was named *Great Snipe*, but this was changed to *Golden Fleece* in September 1937. It was altered again to *Dwight D. Eisenhower* in September 1945. The locomotive was one of six A4s preserved after withdrawal.

Gresley-designed Class A3 4-6-2 locomotive No. 60112 (LNER No. 4481) *St Simon* hauls a set of LNER carriages out of Leeds Central railway station on 17 October 1951. The locomotive entered service in September 1923, named after the 1884 Ascot Gold Cup winner, was rebuilt in August 1946 and withdrawn in November 1964. Leeds Central railway station was opened in 1854 as a joint station between the L&NWR, the L&Y Railway, the GNR and the NER. It replaced the cramped LNW terminus at Wellington Street, which had opened in 1848 with the line to Dewsbury. (YP 1/C596)

In Marsh Lane cutting on 20 November 1951, Class 8F 2-8-0 locomotive No. 48643 is fronting on a coal train. *The LNER Encyclopaedia* states: 'The construction of the Marsh Lane cutting and tunnel through Richmond Hill led to the loss of many lives ... Eventually the line was widened and the tunnel opened out in 1894. This was primarily to allow increased traffic movements after Neville Hill engine sheds were expanded. The opening out of the tunnel resulted in the most impressive civil engineering along the line, with a deep cutting and a series of impressive cross bridges. Neville Hill depot is located just north of the line, east of the cutting.' (YP 1/C604)

Forty-nine Class A1 4-6-2 locomotives were built to the designs of Arthur Peppercorn (who was the LNER's last CME) during the early BR era. However, they were all scrapped with the discontinuation of steam, with none of the original production run surviving into preservation. The locomotives were designed to cope with the heaviest passenger trains in the post-war period on the East Coast Mainline (London–York–Newcastle–Edinburgh–Aberdeen), which consisted initially of trains with up to fifteen coaches and up to 550 tons. The forty-nine engines were built at the Eastern Region's Doncaster and Darlington works between 1948 and 1949. Darlington-built A1 No. 60134 *Foxhunter* with a plain chimney is reversing into Copley Hill on 22 November 1951. *Foxhunter* was in service from November 1948 to October 1965. Its last shed was 50B, Leeds Neville Hill. (YP 1/C605)

The *Queen of Scots* Pullman train en route from Glasgow to London pulls away from Leeds, hauled by Class A1 4-6-2 locomotive No. 60119 *Patrick Stirling*. Fitted with the flared top chimney, the engine is displaying the pre-1957 BR lion logo. On *www.kentrail.org.uk*, it is stated: '[The] *Queen of Scots* [Pullman service ran from] Kings Cross to Glasgow Queen Street, 1st May 1928 to 3rd September 1939, 5th July 1948 to 13th June 1964. Reversed at Leeds and continued thereafter via Harrogate.' Pullman trains were mainline luxury railway services that operated with first-class coaches and a steward service, provided by the British Pullman Car Company. (YP. 1/C664)

Fowler-designed Royal Scot Class 4-6-0 locomotive No. 46137 *The Prince of Wales Volunteers (South Lancashire)* is passing Farnley with a Liverpool–Newcastle train. Built by NBL Co., Glasgow in October 1927, the locomotive was later rebuilt in common with the rest of the class, with tapered boiler and curved smoke deflectors. The South Lancashire Regiment (The Prince of Wales's Volunteers) was a regiment of the British Army. It was formed in 1881 by the amalgamation of: the 40th (2nd Somersetshire) Regiment of Foot and the 82nd (Prince of Wales's Volunteers) Regiment of Foot. From 1881 to 1938 it was formally called 'The Prince of Wales's Volunteers (South Lancashire Regiment).' (YP. 2/744s)

An interesting variety of carriages trails behind Thompson-designed Class B1 4-6-0 locomotive No. 61372, reversing at Leeds Central railway station on 17 October 1951. Introduced in 1942, the first B1, No. 8301, was named *Springbok* in honour of a visit by Prime Minister of South Africa, Field Marshal Jan Smuts. The first forty of the class were named after breeds of antelopes and the like. The LNER built 274 and British Railways built 136 after nationalisation in 1948. No. 61372, built by the NBL Co., was in service from December 1950 until June 1965. Its last shed was 40E, Langwith Junction. (YP. 2/C596)

On 20 November 1951, Class A3 4-6-2 locomotive No. 60092 (LNER 2746) *Fairway* powers a Newcastle–Leeds–Liverpool express in Marsh Lane Cutting. Built as an A3 at Doncaster in November 1928, the locomotive received a double chimney in November 1959 and trough deflectors in October 1961. The carriages include a Gresley brake third and a Thompson transverse corridor vehicle. The locomotive's last shed was 52A, Gateshead, before withdrawal in October 1964. In subsequent months it was cut up at Drapers, Hull. (YP. 2/C604)

Class A3 4-6-2 locomotive No. 60083 *Sir Hugo* is hauling a Newcastle–Liverpool train of late LNER carriages into Leeds on 12 December 1952. Built as an A1 by the NBL Co. in December 1924, the locomotive was rebuilt to Class A3 in December 1941. A double chimney was added in September 1959 and trough deflectors in February 1962 before withdrawal in May 1964. In common with *Fairway* (illustrated above), *Sir Hugo*'s last shed was 52A, Gateshead, though it was cut up at Hughes Bolckows, North Blyth. (YP. 3/C674)

The War Department (WD) 'Austerity' 2-8-0 was a heavy freight locomotive introduced in 1943 for war service. A total of 935 were built. The NBL Co. was responsible for 545 and the Vulcan Foundry of Newton-le-Willows 390. After the end of the Second World War, the War Department disposed of 930 locomotives. With the creation of BR, 733 of the locomotives were allocated and renumbered into the 90000–90732 series. WD Austerity No. 90640 is seen here with a freight train in Marsh Lane Goods Yard on 15 November 1951. It is displaying shed code 24C, Lostock Hall. Partly visible on the left is Class J77 0-6-0T locomotive No. 68436. (YP. 4/C603)

The Ivatt Class 2 2-6-2T was a class of light 'mixed-traffic' locomotive introduced in 1946. A total of 130 engines were built. Ten were constructed by the LMS before nationalisation in 1948, and were numbered 1200–9. British Railways added the prefix '4' to their numbers, so they became 41200–9. A further 120 were built by BR, numbers 41210–329. Most emerged from Crewe but the last ten were erected at Derby. Fifty engines were fitted with push-pull equipment. No. 41255, built at Crewe in November 1949, is at Holbeck High Level on 22 November 1951. (YP. 4/C605)

A total of seventy-six Gresley-designed D49s in three main variants were built between 1927 and 1935. The D49/1 had conventional piston valves and twenty-eight emerged in three batches between 1927 and 1929. The D49/2 featured rotary cam-operated Lentz poppet valves and forty-two appeared between 1929 and 1935. Class D49/2 4-4-0 locomotive No. 62752 *The Atherstone* is at Copley Hill, Leeds. Built at Darlington in July 1934, it is displaying shed code 50D, Starbeck, its last shed before withdrawal in July 1958. The Atherstone Hunt, with hunting country of around 400 square miles (1,000 km) within Warwickshire, Leicestershire and Staffordshire, was established in 1815 in Witherley, and was known as the Atherstone hounds. (YP. 4/C607)

Class A3 Pacific 4-6-2 locomotive No. 60083 *Sir Hugo*, with a GNR tender, is reversing at Leeds City railway station on 12 December 1952. Shed code 52A, Gateshead, is clearly visible. The first rationalisation of Leeds' railway stations occurred in 1938, when two stations (New and Wellington) were combined to form Leeds City station. This project also saw the construction of the North Concourse and the Queens Hotel. Further remodelling of the site took place in 1967, when all traffic using Central station was diverted into the City station, with it becoming the single main railway station serving the city. (YP. 4/C674)

The LMS Class 4 2-6-0 locomotive was primarily designed for medium freight work, but was also widely used on secondary passenger services. The LMS built 162 locomotives between 1947 and 1952, but only three were built by the LMS before nationalisation in 1948. Designed by H. G. Ivatt, they were classified 4F by the LMS and 4 by BR. No. 43130 is travelling from the Scarborough direction and crossing the ECML at York with a freight train on 29 December 1952. The 'cross-over' has since been removed. (YP. 4/C677)

Class A1 4-6-2 locomotive No. 60116 *Hal O' The Wynd*, with lipped chimney, is on its way to Leeds Central, 8 October 1951. The plume of steam at the safety valve tells us that the locomotive has plenty of power ready to work the *Queen of Scots* Pullman service. The locomotive entered traffic from Doncaster Works during October 1948. It is displaying shed code 52B, Heaton, but its last allocation was 52A, Gateshead, before withdrawal in June 1965. (YP. 5/C594)

Appearing in 1926, the J39 was essentially a J38 with larger driving wheels, designed for freight work. It became the new LNER Group Standard 0-6-0 goods locomotive and a total of 289 J39s were built over fifteen years, making it the most numerous of Gresley's designs. All passed into BR ownership in 1948 and they were numbered 64700–64988. None has survived to preservation. No. 64850 is at Marsh Lane Cutting/Neville Hill on 20 November 1951. (YP. 5/C604)

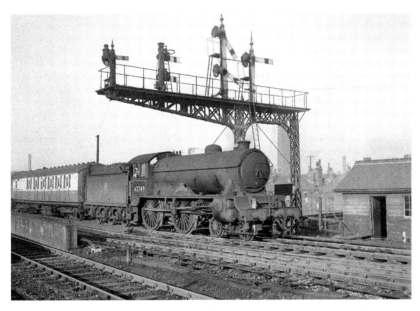

Built at Darlington in August 1933, Hunt Class D49/2 4-4-0 locomotive No. 62749 *The Cottesmore*, with a NE 4125 gallon tender, is at Holbeck Low Level before arriving into Leeds from Harrogate on 22 November 1951. At this time it was a mere seven years away from withdrawal, its last shed allocation being 50B, Leeds Neville Hill. One locomotive in the class, D49/1 No. 62712 *Morayshire*, has been preserved on the Bo'ness & Kinneil Railway. (YP. 5/C605)

Hurrying through Kirkstall on its way from Leeds to Bradford with an evening commuter train in 1952 is Black Five 4-6-0 locomotive No. 44658, built at Crewe in May 1949. Kirkstall railway station, seen in the background, was opened by the MR in 1846 and closed on 22 March 1965. No. 44658's last shed allocation before withdrawal in November 1967 was 10A, Wigan Springs Branch. The Black Five was introduced by William Stanier in 1934 and 842 were built between then and 1951. Members of the class survived until the last day of steam on BR in 1968 and eighteen are preserved. (YP. 5/C642)

Johnson's 0-6-0 locomotives were built between 1875 and 1908 by the MR. Under locomotive superintendents Samuel W. Johnson and Richard Deeley, they ordered 935 goods tender engines of 0-6-0 type, both from the railway's own shops at Derby and from various external suppliers. Although there were many (mostly small) variations between different batches, both as delivered and as successively rebuilt, all 935 can be regarded as a single series, one of the largest classes of engine on Britain's railways. The locomotives rebuilt with Belpair boilers served as late as 1964, but none of them now survive. No. 58212 (without its original tender) is at Stourton on 31 July 1952. Its last shed before withdrawal in March 1956 was 20C, Royston. (YP. 5/C649)

H. A. Ivatt's N1 0-6-2T design was for locomotives to haul the suburban London trains. The first N1, No. 190 (seen here in BR days), was built at Doncaster in April 1907 but proved too heavy for the Metropolitan Widened Lines, and was quickly moved to the West Riding. Built with a number of design changes, the rest of the class appear to have been a success, as by 1912 a total of fifty-one N1s were operating in the London area. All were fitted with condensing gear, except for four which were intended for use in the West Riding. In the north, the N1s were used on short passenger workings. They also worked regularly as station pilots in Leeds and Wakefield. No. 69430 is at Leeds Central station in the early 1950s, withdrawal coming in December 1956. (YP. 6/C596)

Jubilee Class 5XP 4-6-0 locomotive No. 45709 *Implacable* (built at Crewe June 1936) and Royal Scot 4-6-0 No. 46137 *Prince of Wales's Volunteers* (built in October 1927 by the NBL Co.) are at Leeds City railway station with a Leeds–Liverpool train on 12 December 1952. No. 45709 is displaying shed code 9A, Longsight (Manchester), and the fireman appears to be altering the head lamps. (YP. 6/C674)

The Flying Scotsman service ran between London and Edinburgh from 1862. It was initially titled the Special Scotch Express and the original journey took 10½ hours, including a half-hour stop at York for lunch. In 1924, the LNER officially renamed the 10:00 Special Scotch Express the Flying Scotsman, its unofficial name since the 1870s. On 29 December 1952, the 'Up' Flying Scotsman, fronted by grime-coated Class A1 4-6-2 locomotive No. 60145 *Saint Mungo*, is about to travel over the Scarborough lines at the one-time flat crossing at York. (YP. 6/C677)

Class B1 4-6-0 locomotives allocated to Neville Hill, Leeds were used on secondary services radiating from the city, i.e. to Hull, Scarborough, York and Stockton. In both 1952 and 1962 Neville Hill had eight B1s. No. 61020 *Gemsbok*, hauling old Gresley LNER carriages, passes Marsh Lane on a Leeds–Hull train on 20 November 1951. The locomotive was in a batch of thirty built at Darlington in 1946/1947 and its last shed was 50A, York North, before withdrawal in November 1962. Also on view is W. Worsdell Class J77 (NER Class 290) 0-6-0T locomotive No. 68436. This locomotive's last shed was 50B, Neville Hill. (YP. /C604)

Class A3 Pacific 4-6-2 locomotive No. 60112 *St Simon* was allocated to Copley Hill, Leeds, shed three times during its life span: December 1943, June 1950, and April 1951. Built as an A1 at Doncaster in September 1923, it was rebuilt to A3 in August 1946. The locomotive is pictured on 17 October 1951 with a GN coal rail tender and prior to being converted from right- to left-hand drive in October 1952. Its final shed allocation was 35A, New England, prior to withdrawal in December 1964. *St Simon* is heading a Leeds–London train while Gresley-designed J50/4 0-6-0T locomotive No. 68988 shunts empty stock in the background. The 0-6-0T was a popular locomotive, especially for shunting but also for freight work, branch passenger services and even occasional passenger duties. (YP. 7/C596)

The B1s replaced GNR, GCR and NER Atlantics, various GCR 4-6-0 classes and 4-4-0s from all the constituent LNER companies. In LNER days and into early BR days, the class was largely concentrated in local areas. There were plenty in East Anglia and the Great Central area and north-east England had considerable numbers. They were well-used between Edinburgh and Glasgow, between Edinburgh and Carlisle over the Waverly Route, and between Newcastle and Carlisle, and following nationalisation they worked more widely across the system than hitherto. Class B1 4-6-0 locomotive No. 61069 approaches Marsh Lane Cutting with a Hull–Leeds train on 15 November 1951. Two B1s are preserved: 61264, which was rescued from Barry scrapyard, and 61306, the last survivor in normal service, which was purchased direct from BR in 1967 and named *Mayflower*. (YP. 7/C603)

A Leeds–Liverpool train (with LNER stock at the front) leaving Leeds City railway station with Jubilee Class 4-6-0 locomotive No. 45709 *Implacable* and Class Royal Scot 4-6-0 locomotive No. 46137 *The Prince of Wales Volunteers (South Lancashire)* at the head on 12 December 1952. Trains ran via Leeds to Liverpool from Newcastle and Hull, and a variant was the Leeds–Manchester Exchange with through carriages to Liverpool. The last five Patriots of Henry Fowler's Patriot class on order, 5552 to 5557, were built with William Stanier's tapered boiler and so became the first of the Jubilee class. A first order of 113 locomotives was made straight from the drawing board. Initially a disappointment, changes to the blastpipe and chimney dimensions helped to transform them. Interestingly, No. 45709, built at Crewe in June 1936, was damaged by enemy action on 10 October 1940. It was finally withdrawn in November 1963. (YP. 7/C674)

Coasting into York, and just passing the 200 miles from Edinburgh mark, on a sunny spring day in 1956 is Class A3 4-6-2 locomotive No. 60065 *Knight of Thistle*. This was one of twenty in the class that were built as A1s by the NBL Co. during 1924. It was rebuilt to Class A3 in March 1947, fitted with a double chimney in October 1958 and trough deflectors in November 1961 and withdrawn in June 1964. Its last shed allocation was 35A New England. In the north, the locomotive was allocated to Doncaster, Grantham and New England sheds, but never to a shed in either Leeds or York. (YP. C927/4)

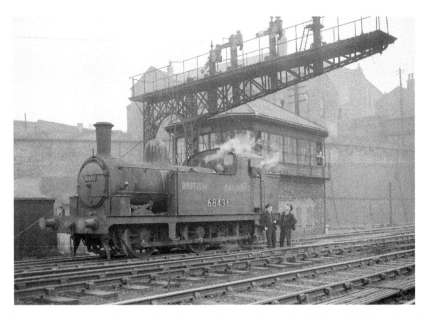

Signalman and assistant, along with other staff, pose alongside W. Worsdell Class J77 (NER Class 290) 0-6-0T locomotive No. 68436, still displaying the British Railways lettering, at Marsh Lane signal cabin, Leeds, on 20 November 1951. Some of the J77s had extremely long lives – No. 954 (BR No. 68392) lasted eighty-six years – but none of the class survived into preservation. (YP. 8/C604)

Heading the Thames–Clyde Express at Leeds station is Royal Scot Class 4-6-0 locomotive No. 46108 *Seaforth Highlander*. Starting from St Pancras, the Thames–Clyde Express travelled by the former MR main line through Leicester as far as Leeds, sometimes with reversals to serve Derby and Nottingham. After another reversal, the train crossed the Pennines to the scenic Settle–Carlisle route, still on former MR territory. Crossing into Scotland, the train used the former Glasgow & South Western Railway's Glasgow South Western Line into Glasgow St Enoch, the city's G&SWR terminus. The train lost its title in May 1975 when the West Coast Main Line was electrified, but the service continued to run until 1976. (YP. 8/C594)

In 1898 the NER needed an enlarged 4-4-0 locomotive, which quickly resulted in Wilson Worsdell's Class R (LNER D20) locomotives. They used a variety of design features that Wilson Worsdell had used on previous locomotives and quickly proved very successful. The initial batch of ten was built in 1899, followed by two more batches of ten each in 1900–1. A further three batches of ten each were built in 1906–7. All sixty D20s were built at Gateshead. Class D20/1 No. 62397, built in September 1907, is fronting a Leeds–York train in Marsh Lane Cutting on 15 November 1951. It is also carrying a rebuilt tender. The locomotive's last shed allocation was 53D, Bridlington, before withdrawal in February 1957. (YP. 8/C603)

A passenger train hauled by Black Five 4-6-0 locomotive No. 44828, built at Crewe in July 1944, is passing Holbeck Low Level on 22 November 1951. It is displaying shed code 20A, Leeds (Holbeck), which was its last allocation before withdrawal in September 1967. Holbeck station was unusual in that it had platforms on two different levels, the Holbeck High Level (HL) and the Holbeck Low Level (LL). The low-level platforms were closed to the public in 1958 and the high-level platforms succumbed to closure shortly afterwards, in 1962. (YP. 8/C605)

Pictured at Harrogate on 29 November 1951, this member of the Hunt Class of 4-4-0 locomotives was unique. It was rebuilt by Thompson in August 1942 from D49/2 with three cylinders instead of two of D11 pattern, along with Stephenson valve gear and piston valves. Reclassified D49/4, it was the only member of the class. No. 62768 *The Morpeth* was built at Darlington in December 1934 and withdrawn on 3 November 1952 from 50D, Starbeck shed, after being damaged in a collision. In subsequent months it was cut up at Darlington Works. Note the NER water crane on the left. (YP 8/C608)

The GCR Class 8K 2-8-0 locomotive was designed by John G. Robinson and introduced in 1911 for heavy freight. Sir Sam Fay ensured that it became the standard military locomotive during the First World War as the ROD 2-8-0, which was used by the Railway Operating Division of the Royal Engineers. Thus 521 ROD locomotives were built, of which 273 were purchased by the LNER during the early 1920s. The LNER classified the 8K as a major part of its LNER Class O4, the original builds being class O4/1. Class 04/1 2-8-0 locomotive No. 63584 passes Wortley South, Leeds, on 13 January 1957 with a slow freight train. Withdrawal of all O4 and O1 locomotives commenced in 1959 and was completed by 1965. The engine on the left is a J50 tank.

Locomotives Illustrated No. 34 states: '[The Hunts] were essentially NER locomotives working most of their lives in Yorkshire and further north – nothing really to tax a modern engine since their duties were largely on secondary passenger work. The Leeds allocation, however, rose to higher things on the daily Glasgow express which they worked to and from Newcastle.' Built at Darlington in July 1934, Class D49/2 4-4-0 locomotive No. 62755 *The Bilsdale* is running light engine at Leeds on 8 October 1951. It is displaying the code of its August 1950 shed allocation, 50D, Starbeck, where a total of thirteen D49s were based at that time. The locomotive's last shed before withdrawal in November 1958 was 50C, Selby. (YP. 9/C594)

Peppercorn Class A1 4-6-2 locomotive No. 60123 *H. A. Ivatt* backs light engine out of Leeds Central station on 17 October 1951. The locomotive was built at Doncaster in February 1949, but was not named (after GNR locomotive engineer Henry Alfred Ivatt, 1851–1923) until July 1950. The original allocation of A1s when they entered service sent five to Copley Hill, Leeds. Three years later, when a major reallocation took place, Copley Hill received ten A1s. No. 60123 was originally placed at 36A, Doncaster, then moved to 37A, Ardsley, before withdrawal in October 1962 after an accident. (YP. 9/C596)

Built at the Vulcan Foundry in March 1935, Stanier-designed Black 5 4-6-0 locomotive No. 45078 is light engine at Neville Hill West box on 20 November 1951. Note that it is displaying BR lettering on the tender. Earlier, in 1948, the locomotive was allocated to 25G, Farnley Junction, but ended its days at 5B, Crewe South, before withdrawal in December 1965. As well as working main-line trains, Class 5s worked summer specials from the West Riding to Whitby, via York, Malton and Pickering. (YP. 9/C604)

The GNR's 521 Class of 0-6-0 steam locomotives was introduced in 1911. They were designed by Henry Ivatt for goods traffic. From 1912 to 1922 further examples, slightly modified by Nigel Gresley, were built and designated 536 Class. The LNER classified them both as J6. No. 64208, built at Doncaster in July 1913, is with a freight train at Holbeck High Level on 22 November 1951. A storm sheet is visible on the cab roof. The locomotive's 1948 shed allocation was 37A, Ardsley, and it was withdrawn from there in April 1961, returning to Doncaster, its birthplace, to be cut up. None of the Class has been preserved. (YP. 9/C605)

The LMS Compound 4-4-0 was designed by for passenger work. After Grouping, 195 were built by the LMS, adding to the forty-five MR 1000 Class, to which they were almost identical, apart from the driving wheel diameter being reduced from 7 feet on the Midland locomotive to 6 feet 9 inches on the LMS version. They were given the power classification 4P. The LMS continued the Midland numbering from 1045 to 1199, and then started in the lower block of 900–39. After nationalisation in 1948, BR added 40000 to their numbers. Built at Derby in November 1924, Compound No. 41080 is at Leeds Central railway station on 8 October 1951. At this time, it was less than three years away from withdrawal in January 1954; its last shed was 20E, Manningham. Except for the first of the Midland 1000 Class engines, none has survived to preservation. (YP. 10/C594)

Peppercorn's Class A1 Pacific 4-6-2 locomotives were built at Doncaster (nos 60114–60129, 60153–62) and Darlington (nos 60130–52) all appearing between August 1948 and December 1949. Emerging from Darlington in June 1949, No. 60150 was not named *Willbrook* until January 1951. It is leading a Newcastle–King's Cross train into York with 'Hunt' Class D49 4-4-0 locomotive No. 62753 *The Belvoir* to the left on 29 December 1952. The A1 had adopted the BR Brunswick green livery earlier in January and has the plain double chimney. During its lifespan it was based at 52B, Heaton; 52A, Gateshead; and 50A, York, before withdrawal in October 1964. (YP. 10/C677)

Entering traffic in December 1951 from Horwich Works, Class 4F 2-6-0 locomotive No. 43126 trundles across Selby Swing Bridge on 31 October 1962. The bridge, constructed for the NER under the supervision of Thomas Eliot Harrison, opened in 1891.

Built at Doncaster in 1948, Peppercorn Class A1 Pacific 4-6-2 locomotive No. 60120 *Kittiwake* (six A1s took their names from birds) is light engine at Wortley South GN signal box on 17 October 1951. Initially allocated to King's Cross, the locomotive moved to Copley Hill in June 1950 and then to York in September 1963 before withdrawal in January 1964. The A1s were renowned for reliability and by 1961 the class had accumulated 48 million miles, equivalent to 202 miles per locomotive each calendar day. These were unmatched by any other steam locomotive on BR. (YP. 11/C596)

The first three H. G. Ivatt-designed 4F (later 4MT) engines were numbered 3000–2 by the LMS, but became 43000–2 when renumbered by BR – 40000 was added to the running number to indicate an ex-LMS locomotive. The remaining 159, built by BR, continued the number sequence: 43003–161. Construction was divided between different locations: seventy-five were completed at Horwich Works, fifty at Doncaster Works and thirty-seven at Darlington Works. The class was also sometimes called 'mucky ducks', 'doodle-bugs' or even 'Flying Pigs'. No. 43097 leaves York with a passenger stock. (YP. 11/C677)

The *Queen of Scots* Pullman leaves Leeds and heads north behind Doncaster-built Class A1 4-6-2 locomotive No. 60116 *Hal O' The Wynd* on 4 October 1951. The picture is taken from Wortley signal cabin. Initially allocated to Heaton shed in 1948, the locomotive moved to Tweedmouth (September 1962) and Gateshead (October 1964) before withdrawal in June 1965. The Pullman Car Company had its own workshops at Brighton, though vehicle manufacture was also carried out by Birmingham Railway Carriage & Wagon Company and Metropolitan Cammell Carriage & Wagon Co. The London, Brighton & South Coast Railway was the first UK railway company to operate a complete Pullman train, the Pullman Limited, which started on the London to Brighton route on 5 December 1881. (YP. 12/C593)

Smoke from the engine, seen in the bottom of the picture, slightly obscures the view of the *Queen of Scots* Pullman train drawn by Darlington-built Class A1 4-6-2 locomotive No. 60139 *Sea Eagle* at Wortley South on 17 October 1951. Upon nationalisation in 1948, the contracts the PCC had made with the various railway companies to operate services over their lines were continued by BR. But the PCC remained privately owned. During the Second World War, all Pullman services were suspended. They were restarted shortly thereafter. By the late 1950s the image of Pullman trains remained luxurious, but the rolling stock was increasingly outdated. The PCC was bought by the public body the British Transport Commission (BTC) in 1954. *Sea Eagle* was withdrawn in June 1964; its last shed was 36A, Doncaster. (YP. 12/C596)

Built in April 1935 by the NBL Co., William Stanier-designed Jubilee Class 4-6-0 locomotive No. 45605 was named *Cyprus* in July 1936. It is with an Edinburgh–Leeds–London St Pancras train coasting into Leeds on 4 October 1951. The Jubilee class ran with three basic tender patterns: Fowler 3,500 gallon, Fowler high-sided (10 off) and Stanier 4,000 gallon. However, taking into account rivets, wheelbase and welds, this can be subdivided into a total of eight patterns. *Cyprus* was allocated to 20A, Leeds Holbeck, in 1948, 1950 and 1957, and was withdrawn in February 1964. A month later it was transferred to 17B, Burton, and then cut up at Crewe Works. Note the look-out man standing under the signal post. (YP. 13/C593)

The LMS's Class 8F 2-8-0 locomotive was designed for hauling heavy freight. Between 1935 and 1946, 852 were built (not all to LMS order) as a freight version of William Stanier's successful Black Five and the class saw service overseas during the Second World War. The 8F design incorporated the two-cylinder arrangement of the Black Fives. They were initially classified 7F, but this was later changed to the more familiar 8F. No. 48158 is with a freight train and has a snow plough attachment at Wortley on 4 October 1951. The lamps indicate Class E: Express freight with no less than four fitted vehicles attached to the locomotive. No. 48148 is also displaying shed code 20A, Leeds (Holbeck). It was later allocated to 16A, Nottingham, from where it was withdrawn. (YP. 14/C593)

The A2/2 class of locomotives were former members of Sir Nigel Gresley's P2 Class. Appointed in 1941, Edward Thompson decided to rebuild the P2 Class, changing the wheel arrangement from 2-8-2 to a 4-6-2 configuration. All the P2s were rebuilt at Doncaster during 1943–4, becoming nos 60501–60506 with BR. The Thompson Pacifics all featured a chassis which positioned the cylinders unusually, between the rear bogie wheel and the front driving wheel. No. 60502 *Earl Marischal*, leaving York with a King's Cross–Newcastle Express on 29 December 1952, was the last of the A2/2s to go, being withdrawn from 50A, York North, at the beginning of July 1961. Later in the month it was cut up at Doncaster Works. *Earl Marischal* was the only A2/2 to cover over one million miles in service, 360,907 as a P2 and 673,947 as an A2/2.

Gresley-designed Class A4 4-6-2 locomotive No. 60029 *Woodcock* is at Copley Hill, Leeds, on 1 August 1952. Built at Doncaster in July 1937, *Woodcock* went through seven colour changes: green (originally); blue (July 1938); black (September 1942); blue (June 1947); purple (July 1948); blue (January 1950); and green (October 1952). The locomotive was withdrawn from 35A, New England, in October 1963 and cut up at Doncaster in January 1964. Leeds Copley Hill shed closed in the same year. (YP. 15/651)

Entering service from Darlington in October 1943, V2 Class 2-6-2 locomotive No. 976 (later 60976) still had its LNER number when this picture was taken in May 1948. The locomotive is picking up water at the troughs at Danby Wiske, Northallerton. In railway terms, a water trough is a device to enable a steam locomotive to replenish its water supply while in motion. It consists of a long trough filled with water, lying between the rails along a flat stretch of railway track. When a steam locomotive passes at speed over the trough, its water scoop can be lowered, and the speed of forward motion forces water into the scoop, up the scoop pipe and into the tanks or locomotive tender. No. 60796's shed allocation in 1948 was 50A, York North, being withdrawn from St Margaret's in September 1966. (YP. 17/258C)

V2 No. 60865, a Darlington-built 2-6-2 locomotive, is passing Copley Hill depot on 2 August 1952. Equally at home on freight or passenger work, a large number of V2s were allocated to both York and Doncaster sheds. Ten locomotives were associated only with these two sheds throughout their existence. By comparison, Copley Hill, Ardsley and Wakefield had very few. No. 60865 was allocated to Copley Hill in 1948, being withdrawn from Gateshead in June 1965. The last V2 was withdrawn on 31 December 1966. (YP. 18/C652)

Doncaster-built Class A1 4-6-2 locomotive No. 60118 *Archibald Sturrock* (named almost two years after construction) is held up while a Bristol train headed by a Class B1 4-60 locomotive gets away from Leeds on 2 August 1952. Interestingly, No. 60118's first allocated shed was Copley Hill; it was also there in January 1955, at Ardsley in 1962 and finally at Neville Hill before withdrawal in October 1965. (YP.19/C652)

Gathering speed, the 10.20 a.m. service to King's Cross leaves Leeds behind Class A4 4-6-2 locomotive No. 60006 *Sir Ralph Wedgewood* on 2 August 1952. Entering traffic from Doncaster in January 1938, the locomotive was originally named *Herring Gull*, the name change occurring in January 1944. The *RCTS Part* 2 states: 'From 1951–1961 ... the A4's did much fine work throughout the East Coast route. Only three sheds housed them King's Cross – 19, Gateshead – 8 and Haymarket – 7. At King's Cross nine or ten were booked to regular crews in the top link working lodge turns to Leeds on the "Yorkshire Pullman", "Tyne Tees Pullman", "Tallisman" and other trains.' (YP. 20/C652)

Built at Darlington in October 1941, Class V2 2-6-2 locomotive No. 60921 is heading into Doncaster on 27 March 1952. Hexthorpe Bridge is in the background. The vast majority of the V2's work was done on the East Coast Main Line and so successful was the overall design that no major modifications were made to the locomotives throughout their working life. No. 60921 was allocated to 36A, Doncaster, in May 1957, withdrawn from there in June 1963 and cut up at Doncaster Works, the graveyard for so many steam locos, shortly afterwards. (YP. l21/C625)

The NER's Class S3 was a 4-6-0 locomotive, designed by Vincent Raven for mixed traffic work and introduced in 1920. The locomotives passed to the LNER in 1923 and were classified B16, some of them being rebuilt: B16/2 introduced in 1937, an LNER rebuild of B16/1 by Nigel Gresley, with his conjugated valve gear; and B16/3 introduced in 1944, an LNER rebuild of B16/1 by Edward Thompson with three sets of Walschaerts valve gear. At nationalisation in 1948, all sixty-nine Class B16 locos were based at York shed. Darlington-built in March 1920, Class B16/2 locomotive No. 61475 (rebuilt in January 1940 and originally No. 61406, renumbered in December 1949) heads a Leeds–Scarborough train in Marsh Lane Cutting on 20 November 1951. The locomotive survived until April 1963, being withdrawn from shed 53A, Hull Dairycoats, and cut up at Darlington. (YP. 9/C603)

An interesting scene at Copley Hill depot, 2 August 1952, with J50 0-6-0T locomotive No. 68911 and two Darlington-built A1 4-6-2 locomotives: Nos 60141 *Abbotsford* and 60139 4-6-2 *Sea Eagle*. *Sea Eagle* was allocated to Copley Hill in July 1951 and *Abbotsford* in May 1950. The locomotives were withdrawn in June 1964 and October 1964 respectively. (YP. 23/C652)

Apart from a number of B1s being fitted with self-cleaning smokeboxes, the locomotives were virtually unaltered during their comparatively short life. Entering service from Darlington in August 1947, Class B1 4-6-0 No. 61033 *Dibatag* is reversing at Copley Hill depot on 2 August 1952. Curiously, the *dibatag* (*Ammodorcas clarkei*), or Clarke's gazelle, is an antelope found in the sandy grasslands of Ethiopia and Somalia. The locomotive was withdrawn from 19C, Canklow, in March 1963. (YP. 24/C652)

Originally named *Osprey*, Class A4 Pacific 4-6-2 locomotive No. 60003 entered traffic in August 1937, but was renamed *Andrew K McCosh* from October 1942. Pictured in Leeds, clearly displaying shed code 34A, King's Cross, it was among the first five A4s withdrawn by BR (60003, 60014, 60028, 60030 and 60033) in December 1962 from the King's Cross shed. All five were cut up at Doncaster.

The Yorkshire Pullman passes Holbeck High Level as it leaves Leeds for King's Cross behind Class A1 4-6-2 No. 60118 *Archibald Sturrock* on 2 August 1952. The decline in the public's use of the Pullman services was partly due to the development of the British motorway network and increasing competition from domestic air travel for the passengers who could afford the Pullman surcharge. But improvements to BR's normal first-class service also had an impact. For example, the Mark 1 Pullmans lacked air-conditioning, while later batches of ordinary Mark 2 stock had this feature as standard in both first and second class. The advent of much faster InterCity 125 trains with new BR Mark 3 coaches also resulted in the demise of the Mark 1 Pullman services on the East Coast Main Line in 1978. (YP 26/C652)

The White Rose service passes Wakefield Westgate with Class A3 4-6-2 locomotive 60046 *Diamond Jubilee*, which emerged from Doncaster as an A1 in August 1924, but was rebuilt to A3 in August 1941. The White Rose ran between King's Cross–Leeds/Bradford from about 1949 to 1964. Wakefield Westgate railway station originally opened in 1867, but was remodelled in the 1960s.

The 2-6-4T locomotives were designed by Charles E. Fairburn for the London Midland & Scottish Railway (LMS). Between 1945 and 1951 277 were built, Fairburn's design being based on the earlier LMS Stanier 2-6-4T. Classified 4P, they were used mainly for suburban passenger trains. Built at Derby in June 1949, No. 42113 is between Leeds Central and Holbeck High Level with a Bradford passenger train on 2 August 1952. The locomotive was withdrawn from 13A, Trafford Park, in July 1965 and cut up at Drapers, Hull. (YP. 27/C652)

A busy scene at Leeds Central railway station featuring Class A1 4-6-2 locomotive No. 60125 *Scottish Union*, an unidentified A1 and two J50 0-6-0T locomotives. *Scottish Union*, built at Doncaster in April 1949, was allocated to Doncaster in April 1949, Copley Hill in June 1950, Grantham in February 1953, Copley Hill in June 1953, Grantham in May 1954, King's Cross in June 1957 and Doncaster in January 1958, withdrawal coming in June 1964. (YP. 28/C652)

The Thames–Clyde Express with Class 5 4-6-0 locomotive No. 44755, featuring Caprotti valve gear and double blast pipe, is at Leeds City railway station on 8 October 1951. The locomotive is displaying the shed code 20A, Leeds Holbeck. No. 44755 was built at Crewe Works in May 1948; its last shed was 9B, Stockport Edgeley, before withdrawal to Crewe in November 1963. (YP. SC 1/C594)

The English Electric company, which had absorbed the engine-maker Napier & Son into its empire in 1942, was a major builder of diesel and electric locomotives. Realising the potential of Napier's Deltic engine for rail traction, the EEC built a demonstrator at its Dick, Kerr works in Preston between 1954 and 1955. Officially numbered DP1 (Diesel Prototype number 1, although this was never borne on the locomotive), it carried the word 'Deltic' in large cream letters on its powder-blue sides. The locomotive is passing Gargave railway station in August 1956. In March 1961, 'Deltic' was withdrawn and donated to the Science Museum, London. It is currently in the National Railway Museum site 'Locomotion' in Shildon, County Durham.

WD 2-8-0 locomotive No. 90518 is at Arthington and displaying head lamp code H: through freight or ballast train. The locomotive was withdrawn from 50A, York North, in February 1966 and cut up at Thomson's, Stockton.

An aerial view, probably taken from Holbeck shed coaling tower, of Engine Shed Junction with a Crewe-built 'Crab' Class 2-6-0 locomotive, No. 42851, at the bottom of the picture. They were noted for their appearance, with large, highly-angled cylinders, caused by restricted loading gauge, which gave rise to the locomotives being known as 'Crabs'. Also to be seen is Derby-built BR Standard Class 5MT locomotive No. 73138. BR built 172 of these locomotives, essentially a development of the LMS Stanier Class 5 4-6-0 (Black Five). Thirty engines, numbers 73125 to 73154, were built with Caprotti valve gear and poppet valves. Holbeck motive power depot is out of view to the left. (YP. H786/6)

Built in November 1924 by the NBL Co. as a Class A1 4-6-2 locomotive, No. 60081 *Shotover* was rebuilt to Class A3 in February 1928. In later years, after unsuccessful trials with very small wing-type smoke deflectors fitted at each side of the chimney, it was decided to fit the A3 class with German-style trough smoke deflectors, which proved most effective but which marred the locomotive's appearance. Fifty-five of the seventy-nine engines were fitted with this type of deflector from 1961 onwards, but No. 60081 was not among them. Pictured emerging from Bramhope Tunnel's north portal on the Harrogate line during February 1958, *Shotover* was withdrawn from 50B, Leeds Neville Hill, in October 1962 and eventually cut up at Doncaster. (YP. B/W 84)

Class A4 4-6-2 locomotive No. 60017 *Silver Fox* is at Selby on 13 March 1953. The first four A4 locomotives built between September and December 1935 included the word 'silver' in their names because they were intended to haul the Silver Jubilee train. *Silver Fox* carried a stainless steel fox near the centre of the streamline casing on each side made by the Sheffield steelmakers Samuel Fox & Company. The locomotive also features heavily in the 1954 British Transport film *Elizabethan Express*. Withdrawal for the locomotive came in October 1963 and it was cut up at Doncaster.

Double-heading an evening train to Liverpool during May 1950, Hunt Class D49/2 4-4-0 locomotive No. 62727 *The Quorn* is with an unidentified A3 on the approach to Arthington. Built at Darlington Works in June 1929, *The Quorn* was withdrawn from shed 53A, Hull Dairycoates, in January 1961 and cut up at Darlington Works. The *LNER Encyclopaedia* website states: 'All three [D49 class] variants shared the same boiler design, and all were fitted with Ross pop safety valves as standard. The boilers were built by Cowlairs, Robert Stephenson & Co, or at Darlington. All had long lives, with the Darlington boilers averaging about 20 years, and the others averaging just under 19 years.' (YP. B/W 11)

Class WD 2-8-0 locomotive No. 90273 is heading a train of tank wagons at Arthington. The locomotive was withdrawn from shed 25C, Goole, in October 1965 and cut up at Drapers, Hull. The *RailUK* website notes: 'Locos Scrapped at Drapers, Hull. – Total 538', a fair number of these being WDs. (YP. B/W 22)

Gresley's design for the 0-6-0 J39s was introduced in 1926, and a total of 289 were built over the ensuing years. All passed into BR ownership in 1948. There were three variants, mainly to denote tender types, and although primarily a goods locomotive, the J39s did make occasional appearances on passenger trains. Approaching Bramhope Tunnel during August 1958, Class J39/1 No. 64934 is displaying lamp code class K: 'Pick up or branch freight or mineral/ballast train on a short haul run'. The locomotive's last shed before withdrawal in December 1962 was 50B, Leeds Neville Hill. None of the class has survived to preservation. (YP. B/W 28)

Class A3 4-6-2 locomotive No. 60074 *Harvester* hauls the Yorkshire Pullman through Arthington in June 1958. The locomotive was built as an A1 by the NBL Co. in October 1924 and rebuilt to Class A3 in April 1928. The locomotive was allocated to Neville Hill in June 1950, fitted with a double chimney in March 1959 and withdrawn from Neville Hill in April 1963.

Class B 16/1 locomotive No. 61478 hauls a Wetherby Race train at Arthington during the summer of 1958. The NER's Arthington–Otley line, extending 3½ miles, was opened on 1 February 1865. The branch left the former Leeds Northern main line by a triangular junction and headed west. The B16/1 was introduced in 1920, an NER design by Vincent Raven with inside Stephenson valve gear. Built at Darlington in April 1920, No. 61478, still with its NER cab, was withdrawn from 50A, York North, in December 1960. (YP. B/W 35)

An excursion train passes a goods train on the loop line between Arthington and Pool during January 1958. (YP. B/W 83)

Class B1 4-6-0 locomotive No. 61084 is at Arthington in 1957. Built at the NBL Co. in October 1946, the locomotive is displaying lamp code C: parcels, fish, livestock, milk, fruit or perishables all XP stock. Besides being built at the NBL Co., the B1s were also constructed at Vulcan Foundry, Darlington and Gorton. No. 61084's last allocation was 50a, York North, and after withdrawal in June 1964 was cut up at Darlington Works. The B1 locomotive to survive the longest was 61002, which ran for twenty-two years and nine months. (YP. B/W 75)

Entering service in June 1937, Class A4 4-6-2 locomotive No. 60012 *Commonwealth of Australia* is with the Elizabethan service at Alne, in July 1959. *Wikipedia* states: '*The Elizabethan* was a daily non-stop service in celebration of the new 'Elizabethan' era of the early 1950s. Departure from both ends [King's Cross and Edinburgh] was in mid-morning, for a teatime arrival. It ran only during the summer months, including in 1953 and 1954. It was able to make the 393-mile journey from London to Edinburgh non-stop by using LNER Class A4 steam locomotives equipped with a corridor tender, enabling a change of crew en route. It also required drivers to take up as much water as possible at the troughs, since the journey called for over 11,000 gallons of it.' No. 60012 was withdrawn from 61B, Aberdeen Ferryhill, in August 1964. (YP. 1/402T)

Class B1 4-6-0 locomotive No. 61256, built at the NBL Co. in November 1947 and withdrawn in November 1965, is heading a York–Leeds passenger train and running easily down the Sutton Cutting at Killingbeck, Leeds. (YP 3/C698)

'Yorkshire's oddest railway to close next month,' ran the *Yorkshire Evening Post* on 10 July 1964, adding: 'The Thistle Line runs from Malton into Ryedale, serving some of Yorkshire's prettiest townships ... Now it has to go. British Rail today announced its closure. It will not be a train. It will be THE train. The Thistle Line has only one – a goods that leaves Malton on Mondays, Wednesday and Fridays, does its leisurely business in the villages and returns at the end of the day.' The above picture, included in the article, shows the train at Helmsley railway station with fireman Dennis Ward climbing aboard to join driver Jim Fawcett in the cab of Class 03 0-6-0 diesel mechanical shunter D2111 (from 12 December 1973 03 111). Right is Peter Gilbert Hughill.

Black Five 4-6-0 locomotive No. 44853, built at Crewe in November 1944, is leaving Stourton, Leeds, with a Bristol Express on 22 April 1953. A number of Black Fives built under BR administration were used as test beds for various design modifications with a view to incorporating the successful modifications in the Standard Classes of locomotives built from 1951 onwards. In art, the locomotive in René Magritte's Surrealist picture *Time Transfixed* is a Black Five. No. 44853 was withdrawn from 20A, Leeds Holbeck, in June 1967. (YP. 1/C695)

A scene at Wortley on 4 May 1956 where a Class 3F 0-6-0T 'Jinty' No. 47367 and an unidentified shunter and WD are visible. The 3F design was based on rebuilds, by Henry Fowler, of the Midland Railway 2441 Class introduced in 1899 by Samuel Waite Johnson. These rebuilds featured a Belpaire firebox and an improved cab. Between 1924 and 1930, 422 Jinties were built by the ex-L&YR Horwich Works and the private firms of Bagnall's, Beardmores, Hunslet, North British and Vulcan Foundry. (YP. C940/1)

Marsh Lane railway station looking westwards, with Leeds City railway station a short distance away. The view is from the top of Marsh Lane station's Railway Street entrance. A station platform sign is visible on the right as an unidentified Black Five locomotive glides past, fronting a freight train. Marsh Lane itself can be seen at the bottom of Railway Street, just beyond the motorcar.

Leeds Central station with two Darlington-built locomotives: Class V2 2-6-2 No. 60864, centre, and Class A1 4-6-2 No. 60133 *Pommern* to the left. On the right is a Metro-Cammell diesel multiple unit. The V2 was withdrawn from 50a, York North, in March 1964, and the A1 was withdrawn from 37A, Ardsley, in June 1965. Leeds Central closed on 1 May 1967.

Class A4 4-6-2 locomotive 60023 *Golden Eagle* slips into York with a special train from Newcastle to King's Cross on 29 December 1952. Entering traffic from Doncaster in December 1936, the locomotive was in the batch, Nos 4482–98, which was built with government financial assistance to help reduce unemployment. After the 'silver' theme adopted for the first batch of A4s, it was the intention to name the subsequent engines after birds. This followed and twenty-five engines carried the bird names, some, albeit, for a very short period.

Class A4 Pacific 4-6-2 locomotive No. 60017 *Silver Fox* is pictured north of York heading the Elizabethan. The 'star' of the 1954 British Transport film *Elizabethan Express* is *Silver Fox*, although the film makes a point of featuring many railway employees: the maintenance men, the driver and fireman and the stationmaster at Waverley Station.

Two

Rail Crashes

The level crossing accident at Lockington, Humberside (now in the East Riding of Yorkshire), occurred on 26 July 1986 when the 09:33 passenger train from Bridlington to Hull hit a Ford Escort van on a level crossing. Eight passengers on the train, and a boy of eleven in the van, lost their lives. The train was made up of a two-car Class 105 DMU unit coupled to a two-car Class 114 unit.

Eleven people were injured and over 200 others had remarkable escapes when the engine and several coaches of a Newcastle–York express were derailed on Monday 5 June 1950, at a point north of York between Alne and Tollerton. Driver Swinnerton, who was among the injured, said he saw a bend in the line; 'after that it was a case of applying the vacuum brakes and waiting for the best or the worst.' A *Yorkshire Post* cameraman, flying over the scene soon after it happened, took this picture of the wrecked train. Travelling cranes and engineering units were sent from Darlington and York and clearance work began almost immediately.

On 5 June 1957 a man was killed and a woman died later from her injuries when a van in which they were travelling was struck by a goods train on a crossing at Hayburn Wyke railway station, 7 miles from Scarborough. The wrecked van was carried 200 yards up the single-line track on the front of the train. The *Yorkshire Post* reported on 6 June 1957 that the crossing was very dangerous. 'It was impossible to see along the railway line because of high banks until one was actually on the line itself. The gates which open into the roadway and leave the line clear at all times are manually operated and have been unmanned since the station was closed last year.'

Two men narrowly escaped death on 23 June 1958 when several railway carriages broke loose from a siding near Lockwood railway station, Huddersfield, ran down a gradient, crashed through buffers and a bridge parapet overlooking Swan Lane and hurtled on to finish up in the station booking hall across the road. Swan Lane was blocked for several hours and traffic was diverted. Two heavy lifting cranes were used to remove the carriages and hundreds of people watched the work, which took several hours. Later, a Huddersfield juvenile court heard that this incident was allegedly the result of a nine-year-old boy releasing the handbrake of a guard's van.

A driver, fireman and guard jumped clear as the train of twenty-one wagons from East Ardsley, Wakefield, ran out of control at 50 mph down the steep incline from Laisterdyke, 2 miles out of Bradford. When the locomotive crashed into the roadway in Dryden Street, off Wakefield Road, it rocked buildings nearby. Nine ambulances and several fire engines were sent to the scene. The driver, fireman and guard were treated for minor injuries. They 'jumped' about a mile from the scene of the crash, where there had been other mishaps. Driver Wilby said: 'I rammed the lever into reverse, but that would not hold.' The locomotive demolished a porter's mess room before plunging into the street, but no one was in the room at the time.

A head-on collision between two lorries left a heavy digger and lorry cab suspended over rubble-strewn railway tracks on 29 July 2002. Caville railway bridge near Howden was devastated by the impact of the collision, which happened less than 10 miles from the site of the Selby tragedy a year earlier. A Humberside Police spokesman said: 'The potential devastation that this incident could have caused is unthinkable. Thank goodness there was no train passing at the time and that somebody stopped the lorry from going all the way over.' Fortunately, there were no fatalities amongst the occupants of the road vehicles.

A light engine collided with an empty horsebox and a 40-ton passenger coach on the north side of Harrogate railway station on 7 August 1956. The accident occurred during shunting operations. The coach finished up at an angle of about 40 degrees, with one corner in the unoccupied front room of a house in Nidd Vale Terrace and the other at the top of a 70-foot-high embankment. The engine driver escaped with a shaking and an injured hand. The occupants of the damaged house suffered from shock. Seventy-five-year-old Mr Kirby and his wife told the *Yorkshire Post*: 'We were in the kitchen when we heard a noise like a bomb explosion. Going to the front room we saw part of the railway coach in the room.'

Five people were taken to hospital after two trains collided head-on outside Leeds railway station early on 11 November 1993. The 6.17 a.m. Leeds to Blackpool two-car Sprinter was derailed in the collision with the diesel-electric locomotive pulling the Penzance–Leeds mail train. Both driving cabs were badly damaged, but the drivers were saved from serious injury because they were on the left side of their cabs. Passengers and drivers were taken to Leeds General Infirmary, but none were detained. West Yorkshire Fire Service sent four pumps and two special equipment vehicles and provided emergency lighting.

In 2009, Bridlington author and disaster expert Richard Jones began a campaign to have a permanent memorial erected to the nine victims of the Lockington rail disaster. The memorial was unveiled at Driffield Memorial Garden on 25 July 2010 at 2 p.m., and over 100 people attended the service. A book about the disaster was launched in September 2010 with the blessing of many survivors and relatives.

The Selby rail crash occurred at Great Heck near Selby, North Yorkshire, at approximately 06:13 a.m. on 28 February 2001 when a Land Rover Defender towing a loaded trailer (carrying a Renault Savanna estate car) swerved off the M62 motorway just before a bridge over the East Coast Main Line. The vehicle ran down an embankment, on to the southbound railway track, and was hit by a southbound GNER InterCity 225 heading from Newcastle to London King's Cross at over 120 mph. After striking the Land Rover, the leading bogie of the Driving Van Trailer (DVT) (82221) derailed but the train stayed upright. However, points to nearby sidings deflected it into the path of an oncoming Freightliner freight train, running 20 minutes early (which was within the rules) and travelling from Immingham to Ferrybridge hauled by a Class 66 (66521) locomotive. The two trains collided approximately half a mile (642 metres) from the impact with the Land Rover. The Class 66 freight locomotive overturned onto its left side, sustaining major damage to its cab area and right side, and the first nine wagons were derailed and damaged. Both train drivers, two additional train crew on board the InterCity 225 and six passengers were killed. In addition, eighty-two people suffered serious injuries.

Three

Naming Ceremonies and other Events

The British Rail Class 43 InterCity 125 high speed train power cars were built by BREL from 1976 to 1982. Neville Hill Rail Depot was the scene of the naming ceremony of Class 43 No. 43049 *Neville Hill*, an event that was reported in the *Yorkshire Post* on 28 January 1984.

The picture shows the naming ceremony in Hull on 11 September 1937 of Class V2 2-6-2 locomotive LNER No. 4780 *The Snapper: The East Yorkshire Regiment The Duke of York's Own*. General J. L. J. Clarke, colonel of the East Yorkshire Regiment, draws back the veil to reveal the nameplate. Five V2s were named after regiments and two after public schools. It is argued that more locomotives would have been named had the outbreak of war not intervened. No. 60809 was built at Darlington in August 1937 and out of 184 in the class, eight were named. No. 4780 became BR No. 60809, was withdrawn in July 1964 and scrapped at Swindon Works.

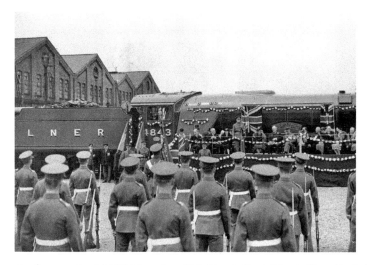

Class V2 2-6-2 locomotive LNER No. 4843 (BR No. 60872) *King's Own Yorkshire Light Infantry* is being named at a ceremony in Doncaster Plant Works on 20 May 1939. The locomotive was completed at Doncaster in April of that year. Of the 184 V2s built, 25 were made in Doncaster. The first battalion of the KOYLI regiment formed the guard of honour at the naming ceremony a few months before their involvement in the war. The V2 locomotive's last shed was 36A, Doncaster, being cut up at the Doncaster Plant Works after withdrawal in September 1963. (YP Rail 22)

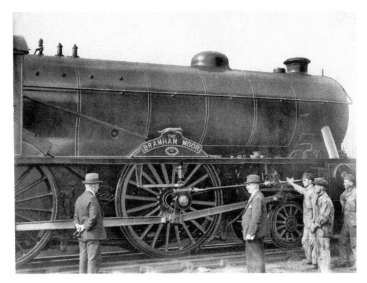

Class D49/2 4-4-0 locomotive LNER No. 2736 (BR No. 62736) *The Bramham Moor* is seen close up in 1932 in Leeds. The D49/2 class, a development of Gresley's D49/1 Class, was introduced in 1928/9 with Lentz rotary-cam poppet valves clearly illustrated here. The D49/2 Class numbered some forty-one locomotives. *The Bramham Moor* was built in April 1932 at Darlington, withdrawn in June 1958 and cut up at Darlington. The last shed was 50D, Starbeck. The Badsworth & Bramham Moor Hounds official website states: 'Foxhounds have been kept at Bramham since 1740 ... The hunt was private until it became a subscription hunt in 1922 ... In 2002, The Badsworth Hunt successfully amalgamated with the Bramham Moor Foxhounds and is now known as the Badsworth and Bramham Moor Hounds.'

V2 2-6-2 locomotive LNER No. 4818 (BR No. 60847) *St Peter's School York, A.D. 627* was pictured at York railway station on 3 April 1939 during its naming ceremony. The locomotive was built at Darlington in March 1939 and saw twenty-six years of service before withdrawal in June 1965. St Peter's School York, founded by St Paulinus of York in AD 627, is one of the oldest schools in the United Kingdom.

Richmond station was the venue for the naming ceremony on 24 September 1938 of Class V2 2-6-2 locomotive LNER No. 4806 (BR No. 60835) *The Green Howard, Alexandra, Princess of Wales's Own Yorkshire Regiment* in September 1938. This was the same month the locomotive emerged from Darlington Works, where 159 of the V2s were built. No. 60835 saw twenty-seven years' service before withdrawal in October 1965; its last shed was 64A, St Margaret's, and it was cut up several months later at Cambells, Aidrie. *Wikipedia* states: 'The Green Howards (Alexandra, Princess of Wales's Own Yorkshire Regiment) was an infantry regiment of the British Army, in the King's Division. Originally raised in 1688, they served under various titles until they were amalgamated with The Prince of Wales's Own Regiment of Yorkshire and The Duke of Wellington's Regiment, all Yorkshire-based regiments in the King's Division, to form The Yorkshire Regiment on 6 June 2006.'

Deltic locomotive D9005 (later 55 005) was named *The Prince of Wales's Own Regiment* at York railway station during October 1963. The ceremony was performed by Brigadier G. H. Cree, colonel of the regiment, on Platform 8 South; those watching the ceremony included two First World War VC holders. Afterwards, the locomotive drew the 10 a.m. train from York to Lowestoft, pulling out of the station to a fanfare from an Army bugler. Brig. Cree presented a plaque with the regiment's crest for Driver Talbot to hang in the cabin. In 1958, the West Yorkshire Regiment amalgamated to form the Prince of Wales's Own Regiment. The locomotive was withdrawn on 8 February 1981 and scrapped.

Deltic locomotive No. 55 022 *King's Own Yorkshire Light Infantry* was pushed into the National Railway Museum, York, on 12 November 1980 by a shunting locomotive and was met with two trumpet fanfares and a VIP reception. As a special concession to its future place in the museum, the locomotive had been painted in its original two-tone green. The chairman of the Friends of the NRM, Lord Donne (right), unveiled a plaque commemorating the earmarking of the Deltic for the Museum. Eastern Region general manager Frank Paterson (left) told guests that the Deltics had revolutionised railway passenger working in the 1960s, and the twenty-two-strong fleet had travelled 68 million miles.

On 2 February 1969, steam locomotive enthusiast the Bishop of Wakefield (Dr Eric Treacy) spent brief but happy off-duty minutes examining the famous Class A3 4-6-2 locomotive *The Flying Scotsman* at close quarters. This picture was taken at the Leeds works of the Hunslet Engine Company, where the locomotive was being overhauled. Dr Treacy once travelled from York to Edinburgh on the footplate of *The Flying Scotsman*.

At a special ceremony in Leeds on 22 December 1983, Class 43 power car No. 43 193 was named *Yorkshire Post*. It became the first in the country to be named after a newspaper. *Yorkshire Post* editor John Edwards, left, unveiled the nameplate minutes before the power car left for London. He said: 'I am very proud to be able to join British Rail in this initiative.' British Rail's Yorkshire Divisional Manger, Paul Watkinson, told guests: 'It is fitting that a power car should be named after a newspaper. Railways and newspapers share much in common. They are both in the communications business, speed and care are the essence of their operation, and the products are highly perishable commodities which must be sold immediately.' John Edwards started the 4,500 horsepower engines on the power car and waved it away with a green flag and guard's whistle.

In January 1984, Malcolm G. Barker, right, editor of the *Yorkshire Evening Post*, unveiled and named Class 43 power car No. 43 157 the *Yorkshire Evening Post*. Paul Watkinson, left, Divisional Manager, British Rail, Leeds, is seen presenting Malcolm with a model of the power car, specially numbered, named and mounted as a memento of the event.

Class P2 2-8-0 locomotive No. 2001 *Cock o' the North* is on display in 1934 at Doncaster Plant Works, where it was built in the same year. Designed by Sir Nigel Gresley for working heavy express trains over the harsh Edinburgh to Aberdeen line, the P2s were given famous names from Scottish lore. *Wikipedia* states: 'It was suggested that [the P2s] were not entirely successful, that their eight-wheel chassis was too rigid for the many sharp curves on the route and that the class was too big for optimum utilisation leading to heavy coal consumption. However, it has also been suggested that Gresley's successor, Edward Thompson, made these largely unsubstantiated criticisms in order to justify his rebuilding of the entire class into LNER Thompson Class A2/2 Pacifics during 1943/4.'

The *Yorkshire Post* of 11 April 1984 carried this picture of Class 43 HST No. 43053 being named *County of Humberside*. Pictured are the vice-chair of Humberside County Council, Vic Chapman, and Bob Urie, British Rail's divisional manager at Hull.

Business and civic leaders took part in naming a diesel-electric locomotive on 16 June 1988 in the hope that it would bring job creating investment to Huddersfield. Mrs Nancy Kidd, The chairman of a business organisation, Huddersfield 2000, unveiled the nameplate on the Class 47 locomotive. She is seen holding the nameplate with the Mayor of Kirklees, Councillor John Holt, and BR's provincial manager, David Wharton-Street. Huddersfield 2000 hoped the travelling nameplate would raise interest in Huddersfield and lead to more work in the town as it passed through Newcastle, York, Leeds, Manchester and Liverpool.

It was a double celebration for railway enthusiasts in August 1988 when British Rail named a locomotive after the Keighley & Worth Valley Railway and also promised long-term renovation work on the town's railway station. The Lord and Lady Mayoress of Bradford, Coun. Mr and Mrs Smith Midgley joined supporters on the platform of Keighley station to see the nameplate unveiled on Class 31 locomotive No. 31 444. British Rail allocated the name to the locomotive in tribute to the K&WVR's twentieth successful year. The unveiling was carried out by British Rail's provincial manager for the Eastern Region, David Warton-Street (right) and president of the society Ralph Pover (centre). Mike Hodson is on the left.

On 7 June 1989 the *Yorkshire Evening Post* reported that the Chairman of the England Cricket Selectors, Ted Dexter, had launched a major cricket initiative in Leeds. On the eve of the opening test match in the Ashes series at Headingley, he named a Class 43 power car, No. 43 115, the *Yorkshire Academy of Cricket*. He said that the Academy, at the famous Park Avenue ground in Bradford, was absolutely vital to the future of the county and hoped it would restore Yorkshire to the prominent position they enjoyed many years ago. Earlier, Yorkshire County Cricket Club president Viscount Mountgarrett praised the sponsorship being put forward by BR to help.

Hull port manager Mike Fell proudly sits in the cab of Class 56 locomotive No. 56 039, which was named after the port. Standing in front of the nameplate is Roger Pettit, north-east business manager of Load Haul, the independent freight arm of the railway network. The naming ceremony took place in the King George Dock in June 1994. Speaking during the ceremony, Mike Fell said that the docks complex owed its existence to the Hull & Barnsley and NER companies, which had invested heavily in the port in the nineteenth century.

A. H. Peppercorn was the LNER's last chief mechanical engineer and none of his A1s are preserved. In 1990, a group of people came together to share an extraordinary ambition – to construct a brand new Peppercorn A1 Pacific. They formed The A1 Steam Locomotive Trust, and after nineteen years of incredible effort, that locomotive, No. 60163 *Tornado*, moved under its own power for the first time in 2008. His widow, now Dorothy Mather, is pictured here. On www.a1steam.com, it is stated: 'Pepp's widow, Dorothy – now Dorothy Mather – has been President of the Trust since the early '90s. She has provided enormous encouragement and support to Trust members, particularly Council members, and attended very many of the Trust's events from the cutting of the steel plates for Tornado's frames in 1994 through to the unveiling of Tornado in green livery at the NRM on 13th December 2008. At the latter event, the Trust presented to Dorothy a commemorative album of photographs recording the history of the Tornado project, and particularly her involvement in it.' The *Yorkshire Evening Post* of 14 July 1994 stated that BSD Plate & Profile Products in Whitehall Road, Leeds had begun the giant task of cutting the mainframes, more than 40 feet long, upon which the locomotive would be built. It also added: 'Mrs Dorothy Mather … pressed the controls to start the cutting job, being done by the Leeds arm of British Steel under sponsorship.'

Four

On Shed and Works

Holbeck engine shed was coded 20A until it came under the auspices of the North Eastern Region in 1957, when it was subsequently recoded 55A. A standard MR 'square' roundhouse containing two turntables, each with radiating stalls, it is seen here in a panoramic view in around 1939. The locomotives on view include No. 1428, No. 5621 and No. 177.

The majority of Gresley's Class A3 4-6-2 Pacifics were named after racehorses. LNER No. 2596 (BR No. 60085) *Manna* took the name of the winner of the 1925 Derby and 2,000 Guineas at Newmarket. The locomotive is on a turntable at York in 1932 and was built at Doncaster in February 1930. Its last shed was 52A, Gateshead, before withdrawal in October 1964; it was cut up at Drapers in Hull.

Locomotives standing in Leeman road sidings at York on Sunday 29 May 1949 due to a rail strike over the introduction of 'lodging turns'. These were periods of work or duty, especially among railway workers, which involved sleeping away from home. The *Yorkshire Post* of 30 May 1949 stated: 'The Railway Executive in a statement [29 May 1949] explained that out of 5,430 drivers and firemen at the 12 depots concerned with express services on the King's Cross–Edinburgh route only 96 men or 1.8 percent were involved in the lodging turns, over which the dispute has risen. The average frequency of lodging for these men, it was stated, was equal to about one night per week.' (YP. 9/161k)

Class V2 2-6-2 locomotive No. 60855 at Copley Hill shed *(56C, formerly 37B)* on 1 August 1952. On *www.britishrailwayseries.com*, Copley Hill's location is aptly described: 'The shed was in the centre of a triangle between three running lines, as confirmed by the ordnance survey map – to the north east, there is Holbeck, and beyond that, Leeds central. To the North west, is Armley & Wortley, on the line that heads out towards Bradford. There are two running lines that go south, crossing each over, from the north west to the south east, the Bradford line runs southwards towards Beeston and Beeston Junction, heading to Doncaster, while the main line from Leeds central runs south west of the shed and towards Huddersfield.' (YP. 8/C651)

Class 5 4-6-0 locomotive No. 44689, entering traffic from Horwich Works in September 1950, is on a turntable at Holbeck Shed on 17 October 1951. The locomotive is displaying shed code 27A, Liverpool (Bank Hall), and it was eventually withdrawn from 68A, Carlisle Kingmoor, in March 1967. The last forty-six Black Fives were withdrawn in August 1968 at the end of steam on British Railways. (YP. 4/C596)

Holbeck shed was closed to steam on 30 September 1967, and the buildings and No. 1 type concrete coaling tower, seen on the right, were demolished in 1970. (D711/8)

At Copley Hill shed on 1 August 1952 is Class A1 4-6-2 locomotive No. 60141 *Abbotsford* with Class A4 4-6-2 locomotive 60013 *Dominion of New Zealand* in the background. The A1 entered traffic from Darlington Works in December 1948, the A4 from Doncaster in June 1937. *Abbotsford* was allocated to 37B, Copley Hill, in May 1950 and withdrawn from 50A, York North, October 1964. (YP. 9/C651)

Opened by the North Eastern Railway, Neville Hill shed dates from 1904. It was coded 50B in the British Railway's North-Eastern Region York District until January 1960, being recoded 55H when taken into the Leeds District. Class A1 4-6-2 locomotive No. 60126 *Sir Vincent Raven*, built at Doncaster in April 1949, is at Neville Hill on 27 November 1951. The shed closed to steam on 12 June 1966 and has continued in use as a diesel depot. (YP. 11-C607)

Class A1 4-6-2 locomotive No. 60136 *Alcazar* with Class N1 locomotive No. 69444 just visible in the background at Copley Hill on 1 August 1952. *Alcazar*, named after the winner of the 1934 Doncaster Gold Cup, entered service from Darlington in November 1948. A summary of its shed allocation is as follows: Copley Hill, November 1948; King's Cross, May 1950; Grantham, September 1951; King's Cross, April 1957; Doncaster, 1958; King's Cross, August 1958; Doncaster, April 1959. It was withdrawn from Doncaster shed in May 1963 and cut up at Doncaster Works. (YP. 11/C651)

Class A4 4-6-2 locomotive No. 60029 *Woodcock* at Copley Hill on 1 August 1952. Built in July 1937, the locomotive retained a corridor tender throughout its lifespan, lasting until October 1963. (YP. 17/C651)

Class J50 0-6-0T locomotive No. 68937 at Copley Hill on 1 August 1952. It is displaying shed code 37B, Copley Hill. (YP. 6/C651)

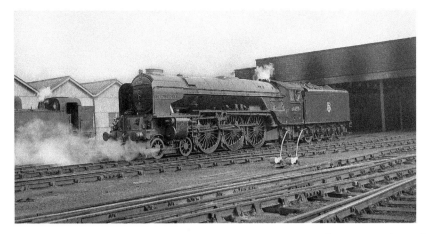

Darlington-built Class A1 4-6-2 locomotive No. 60139 *Sea Eagle* is at Copley Hill on 2 August 1952. Under the heading 'A1 Allocation and Work', *RCTS Part 2* states: 'There was little attempt at regular manning or to book engines to trains at Copley Hill. This shed had four principal through engine workings to London of which only three were worked by Copley Hill men. Two turns were worked on a lodging basis southbound from Leeds ... The third engine left Leeds early morning and returned from London ... This latter out and home daily turn of 372 miles was the longest operated by any Eastern Region crew at that time.' Also in the picture is Class J50 locomotive No. 68911. *Sea Eagle* was withdrawn from 36A, Doncaster, in June 1964 and cut up at Cox & Danks, Wadsley Bridge. (YP. 21/C652)

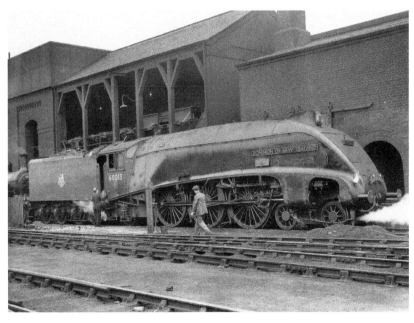

Class A4 4-6-2 locomotive No. 60013 *Dominion of New Zealand* pauses at the Copley Hill coaling plant – one of two not mechanised in the Leeds area – in 1952. The White Rose service board is attached to the front of the locomotive. During July 1950, the locomotive was coupled with a streamlined non-corridor tender but this was changed to a corridor tender in April 1955. The locomotive was in service from June 1937 to April 1963.

'Better prospects for the improvement in railway travel are promised by an increase in supplies of raw materials for the replacement of rolling stock', a *Yorkshire Post* reporter wrote on 13 January 1954. At York Carriage Works (seen above) on the previous day he saw twenty-nine steel coaches under construction where 18 months previously, shortage of materials had brought production to a standstill. Even less than a year ago the output was only one coach per week. In January 1954 this had increased to between five and six per week and the figure expected to continue growing. At that time York Carriage Works covered approx. 62 acres, with 19 acres under roofs, and employed more than 3,000 men.

Between 1988 and 1993, RFS at Doncaster undertook the refurbishment of London Underground (LUL) C-stock used on the Circle, District and Hammersmith lines. The picture shows one of the vehicles entering the New Erecting (E) shop. The work entailed a significant internal refurbishment, including new interior finishes, seats and the opening up of new windows in the intermediate vehicle ends, giving improved visibility and passenger security. The work was undertaken across the RFS site, including body work in (E) Shop and the Light Shop, where much interior work was done.

On 4 February 1993 the *Yorkshire Post* reported that engineers had been working round the clock at Hunslet TPL to find out why gear boxes seized on a new breed of suburban trains, but only when they were running at high speed. 'The firm is building 43 three car units of the new Class 323 trains for local services on the prestigious Manchester Airport rail link ... and the newly electrified cross line in Birmingham,' the *Post* added.

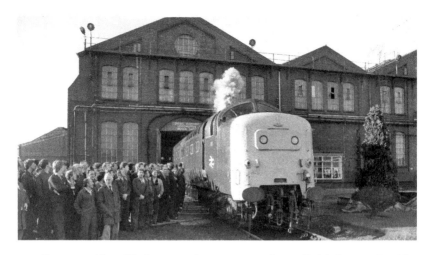

A scene at Doncaster Plant Works on 20 August 1981 where a Deltic locomotive, No. 9009 *Alycidon*, is outside the Crimpsall workshops after undergoing the last general repair to the fleet. The final Deltic run was the 16:30 Aberdeen–York service on 31 December 1981, hauled from Edinburgh by 55019 *Royal Highland Fusilier*, arriving in York at just before midnight. The last train was an enthusiast special, the 'Deltic Scotsman Farewell' on 2 January 1982, from King's Cross to Edinburgh and back, hauled by 55015 *Tulyar* northbound and 55022 *Royal Scots Grey* on the return. Following the farewell, the surviving Deltics were put on display at Doncaster Works before their final journey to the scrap line.

The Channel Tunnel shuttle loco bodies were fabricated by Qualter Hall Engineering of Barnsley and transported to Brush for fitting out. Giving details of the work, *www.qualterhall.co.uk* states: 'Each unit comprised 35 tonnes fabrication, built to accuracy levels which demanded the best of modern manufacturing techniques, in order to achieve the extremely high tolerances required. The complete preparation and painting of the superstructures was carried out at Qualter Hall's own facility at our factory in Barnsley.' This picture of Qualter Hall's works was in the *Yorkshire Post* during February 1994.

Five

Yorkshire's Railway
Heritage Centres

The Elsecar Heritage Railway is made up of a group of volunteers committed to the preservation, restoration and expansion of a preserved railway in South Yorkshire. EHR volunteers carry out all duties on the railway, from driving the engines to maintaining the track. On 1 March 2006, the group signed a lease for the railway from Barnsley Council. The gaining of a lease for the railway was achieved after many years of hard negotiations. The group signed a fifty-year lease of the railway, which was previously managed and funded Barnsley Council. A selection of the EHR's rolling stock is depicted here in September 2006.

The Embsay & Bolton Abbey Steam Railway (E&BASR) is a heritage railway in North Yorkshire (formed in 1968 and reopened in 1979). It is part of the former Midland Railway branch from Skipton to Ilkley (which closed in 1965). The E&BASR currently runs from Embsay via Draughton and Holywell to Bolton Abbey, a distance of 4 miles. Pictured is the original Bolton Abbey railway station.

Bolton Abbey railway station is on the E&BASR. It serves Bolton Abbey, in North Yorkshire, although it is closer to Bolton Bridge. The station, the current terminus of the steam railway, was opened in 1888 by the MR and taken over by the LMS. Despite having a long royal connection, it closed along with the line in March 1965, and the buildings soon became derelict. Following the purchase of the site and associated trackbed by the railway trust in 1995, the station was lovingly restored to its 1888 condition. It was officially re-opened on 1 May 1998 by Sir William McAlpine. Stephen Walker, business manager for the E&BASR, is seen at the newly rebuilt Bolton Abbey station.

Two pictures taken on 31 December 2010 of Tom Ireland, a volunteer fireman and locomotive manager for the E&BASR, with the Great Western Railway 0-6-2T locomotive No. 5643. The E&BASR website states: '[No.] 5643 returned to Embsay at the beginning of November [2010] for another Santa Season, having found favour with the crews and visitors alike the previous year.' On *www.furnessrailwaytrust.org.uk* it is mentioned: 'The 1925-built locomotive was returned to front-line action in September 2006, and has spent the bulk of its operational service since then at the Llangollen Railway where it has been on a rolling annual hire. However this is not an exclusive deal and 5643 has seen action as a star turn at gala weekends and other special events from the Barry Island Railway to the North Norfolk, the East Lancashire to the Severn Valley Railway!'

Pictured at the launch of the *Yorkshire Post* Summer Fun Campaign at the E&BASR on Friday 6 July 2001 are stationmaster Stephen Walker, with, from the left, Sarah Field, dressed as a nun for the Harewood House event 'Sing-a-long-a-Sound of Music', a man in armour from the Royal Armouries and Socrates the Cat from Eureka, Halifax.

Over the weekend of 21/22 September 2002, a 1940s event was staged at Bolton Abbey station by the E&BASR. Several re-enactment societies, including RAF and commando units, pitched tents on the station lawn to create a 1940s military encampment. Business manager Stephen Walker said: 'This is the fourth year we have organised this event and it gets bigger every year.' Over 200 people took part in 2002. The picture shows a re-enactment group marching down the station platform.

Right: Jenny Renn is pictured with strawberries and cream and wearing a China Railways peaked cap on the station platform at the E&BASR on 25 June 2004. She served strawberry teas at a special weekend train on the E&BASR.

Below: Volunteer fireman Beth Furness poses on the footplate of a steam locomotive during December 2003. A picture and an article appeared in the *Yorkshire Post* to publicise the E&BASR, which ran services through the Christmas and New Year holiday period with Santa's Specials on the weekend before Christmas, and Special trains on New Year's Day.

Volunteer ticket inspector Daniel Ferguson, twelve, from Skipton, tastes strawberries in the restored Lancashire & Yorkshire Director's Saloon, dating from 1906, at the E&BASR in July 2002. The carriage was being used in the railway's Strawberry and Wine Specials. The carriage's restoration had been a labour of love for Stephen Middleton (seen on the right) who runs the Working Museum of Luxury Railway Travel from his home in Harrogate. The L&Y Railway built the carriage to provide luxury travel for the company chairman and senior officials, and also to impress celebrities and overseas visitors. It was on its way to the scrapyard in 1965 when it was acquired by the North Norfolk Railway and in a derelict condition when it was given to Stephen Middleton in 1999. The carriage was used in a BBC drama about the son of George V called *The Last Prince*. Stephen said: 'This carriage has an amazing interior, sumptuous first class and charming third.'

On 3 April 1996, there was a historic reunion of the stars of the classic film *The Railway Children*. Jenny Agutter and Sally Thomsett joined their on-screen father, Scottish actor Ian Cuthbertson, for a celebration to honour the Yorkshire location where the film was shot, by unveiling a special plaque. Bradford Film Office had selected it as the recipient of a plaque to mark Cinema 100 – the centenary of British Cinema. It was the first time all three stars had met up since the film was made in 1970. Jenny Agutter, pictured above with Sally Thomsett, said: 'It's a great honour to be here celebrating 100 years of the British film industry and a quarter of a century since *The Railway Children*.'

The Keighley & Worth Valley Railway is a 5-mile (8-km) long former branch line serving mills and villages in the Worth Valley that is now a heritage railway line in West Yorkshire, running from Keighley to Oxenhope. It connects to the national rail network line at Keighley railway station and is currently the only heritage railway that operates a whole branch line in its original form. British Railways closed the line at the end of 1962 as a part of the rail cutbacks of the period. However, a preservation society was formed which bought the line from BR and reopened it in 1968 as a heritage railway. The line is now a major tourist attraction, operated entirely by volunteers. Working on a LMS 0-6-0T Class 3F 'Jinty' No. 47279 around the time of the K&WVR's fortieth anniversary are Gordon Reed and Richard Fairhurst.

The L&Y Class 25 0-6-0 locomotives were introduced in 1876 by William Barton Wright and 280 were built in total. The first was withdrawn in 1930, but then the class remained intact until 1959. The last one, 52044 (L&Y 957), was bought for preservation in 1959 and has been based at the K&WVR since 1965. It starred in the film *The Railway Children* as the *Green Dragon* and is seen in here 2008. It has been used by the K&WVR on summer vintage trains and during special events.

Class 2MT 2-6-4T locomotive No. 41241 steams up the hill towards Haworth station on the K&WVR on 29 December 2002, pulling one of the Mince Pie Specials. The special train services, on which a complimentary mince pie was included in the price of a ticket, began on Boxing Day and ran until New Year's Day. The train featured a 'real ale' buffet car. The tank engine was one of the original locomotives used after the re-opening of the K&WVR in 1968.

Few men achieve their ultimate dream, but railway enthusiast John Wright managed it twice, the *Yorkshire Post* said on 28 January 2002. At weekends the Huddersfield station supervisor for Arriva North changed into a British Rail uniform to work as a steam railways' stationmaster at Keighley – he is pictured here in the ticket collector's kiosk on Platform 4. At the time, he was celebrating thirty years as stationmaster on the volunteer-run Keighley & Worth Valley Railway, which he joined a year after it opened in 1968. John, forty-nine, said: 'I know it's a busman's holiday but I have always keen on railways all my life. I wouldn't like to say which railway is better run but I've no plans to retire from either job.'

K&WVR volunteer Mike Squires watches from the Damems station signal box as the train from Keighley leaves for Haworth, pulled by Class 3F 0-6-0T locomotive No. 47279. When the picture was taken on 29 June 2002, Mike had been Damems' stationmaster for twenty years. He took over when the station was a forgotten weed-strewn halt, but it was lovingly restored with his help and has won awards for best preserved station. Damems originally opened on 1 September 1867 and was closed 23 May 1949, but re-opened on 29 June 1968.

On 1 March 2002 the *Yorkshire Post* announced that steam journeys on the K&WVR were put in jeopardy, as the years had taken their toll on a key piece of equipment. The water column which stood on platform three at Keighley station and provided gallons of essential water to the steam locomotives was about sixty years old and had suffered frost damage. A large crack had formed, from which water leaked constantly. Company chairman Chris Hulme, seen here, said: 'We are seeking specialist advice, but we really need a volunteer to take on this unusual but important project.'

Music writer, promoter and railway enthusiast Peter Waterman could not disguise his love of steam trains when he presented a special Christmas edition of BBC's *Songs of Praise* at the K&WVR on 14 December 2003. He looked over a superbly restored Pullman carriage at Oxenhope station, shouting out details of its history and regaling his audience with stories from his days working with railways. His appearance was an unexpected treat for the many parents who lined up at the station to have their children photographed with him and have him autograph their tickets.

Young railway enthusiast Colin Barron, ten, from Alloa in Scotland came with his family for a day out at the Railfest, York, in May 2004. The event was staged by the National Railway Museum in celebration of 200 years of the train. Colin is seen in the driving cab of a 1958 German rail bus. The Railfest also saw the arrival of the museum's latest acquisition, *The Flying Scotsman*, bought for around £2.5m. The *Yorkshire Post* supported the campaign which saved the loco from being sold abroad, with readers donating £70,000 towards the fundraising appeal.

The *Yorkshire Post* of 19 September 2007 stated that a Second World War steam locomotive, of a type once thought to be lost, 'returned to service on the K&WVR yesterday – complete with a giant tin of spam.' The locomotive was built for the Ministry of Supply by the Vulcan Foundry, Newton-le-Willows, in January 1945. It was returned to service in front of invited guests at the Oxenhope terminus, completing a project that began with its discovery in a forest clearing in Sweden more than thirty-five years ago. Three Worth Valley staff, John Dickinson, Bill Black (Chairman K&WVR, seen here) relaunched it by shovelling a giant replica of a tin of spam into the roaring fire on the footplate shortly after the locomotive arrived at Oxenhope. The restoration project cost around £250,000, the bulk of which was supplied by a Heritage Lottery grant.

Middleton Railway Trust is home to an impressive range of steam and diesel locomotives, some of which date from the nineteenth century. The world's first commercial railway, the Middleton line was built to service the city's developing coal industry. It has since been restored by local enthusiasts to offer a regular service between Moor Road and Middleton Park. Members of the MRT are seen in December 1969 aboard their latest acquisition, a locomotive built by Hudswell Clarke of Leeds, which started life in the mid-1940s shunting at Keighley gas works. Left to right: David Alexander, Bill Greenhaigh, Tim Leech, Charlie Milner and Malcolm Philips. The locomotive had spent much of its life with the Gas Board in Bradford, but had been inactive during the previous three years. The MRT was reported to have bought the locomotive for 'a nominal sum'.

In November 1972, Miss Sheila Young, a teacher at the Dewsbury Road First School, Leeds, became part owner of a 25-ton giant – a 1941 Peckett steam engine. Sheila, whose father and grandfather were both railwaymen, helped the MRT to buy the locomotive. And to record the fact, a plaque was put in the locomotive's cab. On it were the words: 'Sheila's half – Our half'. The locomotive, which cost the Trust and Sheila £720, was delivered to Middleton by road on a low-loader from Preston, where it was used to move freight in a busy yard. MRT members were pictured with the Peckett 1941 0-4-0 tank in the *Yorkshire Post* of 18 November 1972.

The Lord Mayor of Leeds, Councillor William Hudson, waves off a 1909 E. Borrows & Son 0-4-0 WT, No. 53 *Windle*, during a civic visit to the railway on 23 October 1977. The locomotive was one of around twenty similar locomotives which worked at Pilkingtons, based at St Helens in Lancashire. It was donated to the MRT in 1961 and was one of the earliest locomotives to go into preservation. *Windle* was acquired by the Ribble Steam Railway in 2010. It has only worked for ten years out of the last fifty, so the Ribble Steam Railway is looking forward to returning the locomotive to full steam. Only three locomotives of this type survive today.

The regular *Thomas the Tank Engine* and *Postman Pat* events are a big hit with children at Middleton Railway, while older passengers enjoy the trip down memory lane. This picture was captioned in the *Yorkshire Post* of 16 May 2001: 'Postman Pat leaves Greendale to visit Middleton Railway, Leeds.'

Above: Crowds flocked to see a special guest at the MRT on Saturday 31 March 2001. The 'Day out with Thomas' event was one of about 100 being held at heritage steam railways across Britain. The *Yorkshire Post* of 2 April reported: 'Thomas the steam engine gave train rides to families. Fellow engines Percy, Diesel and the Troublesome Trucks also joined in the fun as the Fat Controller kept the engines out of mischief.'

Left: In December 2003, marketing officer Ian Smith is dressed as Santa to promote Santa's steam trains at the MRT.

On Saturday 27 March 2004, members of the MRT and others gathered at a ceremony at Moor Road station in Hunslet, where a Leeds Civic Trust blue plaque was unveiled to mark the railway's contribution to the city. Civic Trust director Kevin Grady, guardian of the city's architectural and industrial heritage, said: 'The Middleton Railway is incredibly important in the history of the development of railways. In 1758 it was the subject of the first ever railway Act to be passed by Parliament and in 1812 it was the first railway in the world to be commercially successful in running steam locomotives.'

MRT volunteers Ian Smith, Steve Roberts and David Monckton celebrate the company's grant of more than £730,000 from the Heritage Lottery Fund on Friday 1 April 2005. The *Yorkshire Post* of 4 April 2005 reported that 'the grant would be spent on a resource centre to display the historic machines. It will include a classroom and other facilities'. Chairman David Monckton said that the grant would be used to significantly enhance public access to the growing collection of Leeds-built locomotives and added: 'We will also be able to tell the story of the Middleton Railway and its connections with the Leeds locomotive building industry together with the story of the preservation of its historic railway by volunteers since 1960.'

'A century after it was built, a Leeds locomotive finally came home', the *Yorkshire Evening Post* reported on 22 April 2006, adding: 'No. 14 a Manning Wardle 0-4-0ST was eased off its transportation trailer and on to the tracks at the Middleton Railway.' The locomotive, originally built in 1912, was the proud possession of Jon Pridmore, who planned to spend £30,000 restoring it to its former glory. Jon, left, and the Middleton Railway vice-president are pictured with the locomotive.

Peter Nettleton, a volunteer at the MRT, is pictured with Hudswell Clarke 0-4-0DM locomotive No. 631 *Carroll*. In the *Yorkshire Post* of Saturday 15 September 2007, Peter said: 'On a cold miserable day in 1969 I'd gone to the huge gas works at Bowling Back Lane in Bradford with a couple of other volunteers from the MRT to see if the locomotive might be any use to us ... When the engine warmed up it was clear that it was in quite good order but just suffering from neglect.' The name *Carroll* is in honour of a Keighley alderman.

The *Yorkshire Post* of Monday 16 April 2007 stated that the MRT engine house and education resource centre had been officially opened at the Moor Road headquarters. Guests included Sir William McAlpine, former owner of *The Flying Scotsman*, who is seen in the foreground. MRT vice-president Ian Smith said the new facilities allowed the trust to enhance public access to the growing collections.

A scene at the opening of the new engine house and resource centre at the MRT. The *Yorkshire Post* picture of 14 April 2007 shows Sir Jimmy Saville waving off the Manning Wardle L Class 0-6-0ST locomotive No. 1210 *Sir Berkeley*, which was featured in the 1968 BBC TV version of *The Railway Children*.

To celebrate the 250th anniversary of the MRT, Leeds Parish Church Choir put on a concert in the Engine Shed under the direction of Dr Simon Lindley with guest Soprano Jenny Leadbeater during June 2008.

The North Yorkshire Moors Railway is the second-longest standard-gauge heritage line in the United Kingdom and runs across the North York Moors from Pickering via Levisham, Newton Dale and Goathland to Grosmont. The NYMR is owned by the North York Moors Historical Railway Trust Ltd and is operated by its wholly owned subsidiary, North Yorkshire Moors Railway Enterprises Plc. It is mostly operated and staffed by volunteers. Mechanics Paul Middleton (right) and Charlie Dore (left) are in the repair workshop at Grosmont station, North Yorkshire Moors Railway, working on Class K1 locomotive No. 62005, built by the NBL Co. in 1949. It arrived at the NYMR in May 1974.

The former Grosmont–Pickering steam railway, which passes through beautiful scenery, was officially re-opened by the Duchess of Kent, seen here, on 1 May 1973. She did so by operating a signal at Grosmont, where she also unveiled one of three plaques. In Whitby, after a trip in a landau, she unveiled a plaque at the Angel Hotel. At the hotel, Sir Mark Henig, Chairman of the English Tourist Board, forecast that the railway would be an important tourist attraction. The Duchess was accompanied by the Marquis and Marchioness of Normanby and Lord Downe, president of the NYMR.

Guest locomotives were among the attractions at the autumn steam gala on the NYMR, the *Yorkshire Post* reported on Saturday 6 October 2001. The gala celebrated the millionth mile travelled by steam locomotives on the historic line, a milestone passed in July of that year. During the weekend, normal passenger services were pulled by a variety of guest locomotives, including A2 Peppercorn-designed 4-6-2 locomotive No. 60532 *Blue Peter*. The interior of the cab is seen above as the driver pulls into Pickering railway station.

In November 2006, volunteers who restore stock from the golden age of travel were hoping railway enthusiasts would snap up their new calendar. *Looking Back* was produced for 2007 by the LNER Coach Association. Based at the NYMR, the association has been restoring wooden-bodied Gresley- and Thompson-designed LNER coaches since 1979. However, restoring each carriage can cost as much as £100,000 and the association relies on donations, grants and sales to keep going. Proceeds from the calendar were to help them continue with their work. Association members Andrew Daniel and John Curtis (secretary) are working on the teak framework of a coach they are helping restore.

The NYMR runs several special events through the year, usually revolving around a particular theme. Local children from Kirbymoorside County Primary School sample the Wizard Event at Pickering station in November 2001 as Jenna Keys (seven) and Jamie Holtby (six) (back) watch from the train as Kiri Keys (five) flies past the train on a broomstick. In the Harry Potter films, the trains and carriages used as the Hogwarts Express were from the NYMR.

Christopher Ware is pictured on the platform at Levisham station on the NYMR, where he was working as the country's first professional artist in residence on a heritage steam railway in September 2007. The aim of the appointment was to open the way for the NYMR to play a greater role in education for adults and young people, and broaden the railway's appeal. Philip Benham, NYMR general manager, said: 'The close association between art and railways goes back a long way. We are sure Christopher's role as Artist in Residence will create huge interest among our visitors.'

'It has taken more than 40 years, but steam returned to Whitby [on 3 April 2007] as the [NYMR] fulfilled its dream of running all the way to the coast again,' wrote the *Yorkshire Post* on 4 April 2007. General manager Philip Benham said: 'We believe the new service will not only be an important attraction in its own right, but will also help the expansion of tourism in both Whitby and the North Yorkshire Moors National Park.' Hauling the train was Class K1 2-6-0 locomotive No. 62005, and it is pictured with driver Dave Gatland.

An unusual market place visitor arrived in Pickering on 21 April 1980 – a locomotive bought as a wife's birthday present. Ex-Southern Railway locomotive No. 34027 *Taw Valley*, rescued from the scrapyard at Barry, was on the last stage of a 25 mph journey by road to the NYMR for restoration. Bert Hitchen of Mirfield, Huddersfield, had bought the locomnotive for his wife Elizabeth. *Taw Valley*'s restoration was finally completed at the Severn Valley Railway in 1987. Spending some time in the maroon livery of the 'Hogwarts Express' as featured in the Harry Potter series of films and novels, the locomotive was used to promote the fourth book, *Harry Potter and the Goblet of Fire*, and hauled a nation-wide tour train with the author J. K. Rowling herself onboard, signing books and giving interviews. However, the locomotive does not feature in the actual films.

The Right Revd Eric Treacy, the 8th Bishop of Wakefield, was remembered on 27 August 2010 when the steam locomotive bearing his name was re-dedicated. Two bishops with links to Wakefield were on hand for the ceremony, the Right Revd Stephen Platten, the then-Bishop of Wakefield, and Dr David Hope, former Archbishop of York and 10th Bishop of Wakefield. Bishop Platten re-dedicated the Class 4-6-0 Black Five locomotive No. 45428 *Eric Treacy* at Pickering station after an eleven-year overhaul costing £600,000 allowed it to return to service.

Six

Staff

Railway staff in Leeds who kept the Inter-City High Speed trains running received framed congratulatory scrolls for their part in the trains covering an amazing 25 million miles in just four years. Drivers, guards and maintenance men were given a hearty slap on the back at Leeds City station in recognition of the success of the East Coast Main Line service and Mr Frank Paterson, British Rail's Eastern Region General manager, handed over the framed scrolls. The distance covered by the train service since they were introduced represented fifty trips to the moon and back, or more than 1,000 miles a day. Mr Paterson is on the right and the others from left to right are: Eric Moore of Bradford, Holbeck depot; Harry Cowling of Whinmoor Leeds, Neville Hill depot; John Fletcher of Burmantofts, Neville Hill depot; and George Hodgson of Halton Moor, Leeds. The four represented all BR staff connected with the 125 trains.

Above: Interior view of Marsh Lane signal box taken in 1951. Note the track layout diagram above on the right.

Below: The work undertaken at the British Railways carriage cleaning sheds at Neville Hill, Leeds, was detailed in the *Yorkshire Post* of 28 May 1953. 'Everyday throughout the year, seven days a week, 111 coaches pass through Neville hill – more in the peak

travel periods of the summer,' explained Inspector R. L. Simpson, who was in charge of all carriage cleaning between Darlington and Doncaster. He said there were five stages of carriage cleaning. The first was to sweep throughout the vehicle, and that happened after each journey. Twice a day, carriages were swept, dusted and the brass work cleaned. Once a day, windows were cleaned, toilets washed and disinfected, and all metal fittings polished. Upholstery was vacuumed regularly and the interiors washed. One of the female Neville Hill cleaners is seen here.

A tablet system to ensure complete safety from collision on the single-line part of the railway between Scarborough and Whitby was illustrated in the *Yorkshire Evening Post* of 28 June 1960. In the picture, a driver is seen handing to a signalman the tablet (inside the satchel) which he has received from another signalman. The driver is also receiving another tablet which enables him to proceed along the next stretch of single line. Without a tablet, a driver was not allowed to enter a section. As only one satchel with the tablet is in the hands of a driver at one time, this ensured that no other engine used the line. This is one of the oldest railway safety systems.

In order to avoid complaints from local residents and to allow testing to be carried out throughout the twenty-four hours of each day, a Test House was built on the Doncaster Plant Works site in 1965. This employed force-ventilated grid resistances to dissipate the energy from locomotives under test. Fully graduated load tests from zero to maximum generator load could be carried out, together with measurements of the output from auxiliary machines. Two locomotives of up to 2,000 hp could be tested simultaneously or, alternatively, one locomotive of up to 4,000 hp. Intercommunication was provided between the Control Room, which was sound-proofed, and the staff in the locomotive cabs. Gerald Nellis (left) and Ronald Smith are pictured at the controls.

In November 1971, *Yorkshire Evening Post* journalist Colin Davison reported that he had 'lived it up' with the North Eastern Region's 'most beautiful member of the catering staff.' This was nineteen-year-old Miss Mari Warner of Bradford. Tired of routine office work, she wanted to travel and became the region's first ever stewardess. Working on the Bradford–London line, which travelled via Leeds, not everyone appreciated her feminine service. 'One gentleman in a bowler hat and pin-striped suit thought British Rail must be going to the dogs if they were employing women as stewards,' she said.

The *Yorkshire Evening Post* of 14 November 1966 ran an article on Standedge's third railway tunnel, completed in 1894, which cut through the Pennine backbone separating Marsden from Diggle, mentioning: 'A team of men were repairing the brick lining of the tunnel some working from a lattice of scaffolding set across the track. Beyond, near a glowing brazier was Jack Smith, the trumpeter of Standedge. He is warned by telephone of a train's approach. He then alerts [any] work gang with a shrill on a whistle for a train on the up line and a blast on a trumpet for a train on the down.' The 1894 double-bore tunnel was opened by the L&WR with double track, and was 3 miles, 60 yards (4,806 m) long.

Mrs R. M. May and Mrs H. M. Glover buy their tickets from Mr George Postill, a guard on the Ilkley train at Leeds. The photograph was included in a *Yorkshire Post* article of 8 October 1968 about pay trains, which had been introduced on three West Riding lines the previous day. Their introduction was not without criticism, but support came from C. H. Wright, chairman of Ilkley Railway Supporters Association: 'You can't have it both ways – manned stations and a service; it is one or the other and we would prefer to have the service,' he said.

Making the Ilkley–Leeds pay train run four times a day, fifty-four-year-old John Cooke won special praise from his passengers in December 1974. 'His cheerful attitude in his duties with comments he makes en route create a very amiable atmosphere to commuters on this line who are generally tired on returning from business,' said Keith Beanlands, district manager of the Pearl Assurance Company, who wrote to British Rail commending Mr Cook's helpfulness to passengers. John of Addingham said: 'I'm cheerful because I have been used to working with the public all my life. I was a conductor on the buses before joining the railway.'

'A new cleaning and servicing depot for trains – the first of its kind on BR has been opened in Leeds,' the *Yorkshire Post* of 8 May 1969 reported. The depot at Neville Hill took over the cleaning and servicing work done at Leeds City station, Bradford Forster Square station, Manningham depot and the two Copley Hill depots. British Rail officials had toured the £500,000 depot the previous day. It had been in use since February. A spokesman for BR commented: 'It does not mean that trains will be cleaned and serviced more regularly, but they should be cleaned more thoroughly.' The photograph shows a push-button console at the west end of the depot. It was one of two that controlled internal movements by signalling and loudspeaker points.

In January 1971, it was revealed that the men who staffed Kirkstall Junction, an outpost beside the lines running into Leeds, had a small duty. It was primitive and slightly distasteful – not at all in keeping with the glossy Inter-City publicity – but there was some consolation in the few shillings overtime they were paid for it. The daily (or nightly) task was to take the spade provided, walk a few yards from the signal box, dig a hole, empty a chemical lavatory into it and replace the topsoil. The overtime involved – a little over an hour in a working week – was 10s 2d (51p).

Featured in a *Yorkshire Evening Post* article of 12 October 1977 on Leeds City station was a short piece about 'one of the faceless voices that echoes across the platforms and concourse ... Mrs Joan Cocker the station announcer'. Joan lived at Wortley, Leeds, and had being doing the job for the previous seven years. In answer to all those critics of BR announcers, Jean said: 'We do our best to sound like Angela Rippon. But I think if she had to sit here she'd be horrified.' At that time the station handled 25,000 passengers daily. Among the employees were 263 parcels staff and porters, 153 clerks, 25 signalmen and 120 guards.

The last Yorkshire Pullman operated on Friday 5 May 1978. Guard Bennet is seen here waving off on the final run. On the following day, the *Yorkshire Post* reported: 'The Yorkshire Pullman has come to be known as the "gentleman's train" leaving Harrogate at a civilised hour – 9.50 am ... Every few miles during the journey through Yorkshire there were photographers waiting to capture the last train on film and someone in British Rail's hierarchy had even provided one of the most apt engines *The King's Own Yorkshire Light Infantry*.'

Bill Addy at the controls of a train on the Leeds–Bradford line, 4 July 1978, and featured in a *Yorkshire Post* article about vandalism.

Burton Agnes' 1903 signal box, a listed building, with relief signalman Raymond Airey on 26 October 1989.

Above left: On Wednesday 18 November 1981, the *Yorkshire Evening Post* stated that Albert Gudgeon, who had served forty-two years on the railways, would book his last ticket on Saturday when he retired. He had been booking office clerk at Selby railway station for the previous twenty-eight years. Albert started his railway career at Wislow railway station as a porter. During the Second World War, he saw action at Dunkirk. After stints at Micklefield and South Milford, he returned to Selby as a booking clerk. 'Meeting people in Selby in my job has been a great experience,' said Albert.

Above right: The Clayton West Branch opened on 1 September 1879 and closed on 22 January 1983. Ron Burdett, a signalman who had worked at Clayton West station for twenty-six years, switched the points of Yorkshire's last branch line. The *Yorkshire Post* of Monday 24 January 1983 commented: 'There's nothing quite like the closure of a railway line to provoke nostalgia and the closure of the Clayton West Branch was no exception ... Locals, some of whom had never travelled on the 103 year old line were joined by enthusiasts who had travelled from all parts of the country to queue for a ride on the last few trains.'

Above left: In February 1985, it was announced that Miss Christine Moss had become the first female operator of the railway swing bridge at Selby. She took a fortnight to master the twenty switches and levers needed to open the bridge. It normally took about six weeks to train as an operator. Christine, of Orchard Lodge Barlby, said: 'On a busy day where there is a high tide suitable for river traffic, I will be called upon to operate the bridge about four or five times.' She had begun working for British Railways as a carriage cleaner in York. 'But this is a higher grade job and I am now classed as a senior rail person,' she said.

Abobe right: During the late 1980s, the railway station at Foulridge, near Colne, was transported to Ingrow West. It was brought across the Pennines stone by stone in a three-year project costing £50,000. In March 1990, it won an Ian Allan Railway Heritage Award for the K&WVR. Stationmaster Stuart Mellin, pictured, is seen on the platform. K&WVR publicity officer Graham Mitchell said: 'It was like a huge jigsaw. I cannot think of another railway station that was picked up and moved stone by stone from another site.'

Seven

Stations, Signal Boxes, Tunnels and Viaducts

Some of Lewis's staff at Leeds City station in about 1958 for an outing to Scarborough.

The Dales Rail, a special charter, began in the spring of 1975. The service set off from Leeds and terminated at Carlisle, dropping its passengers, usually shod in hiker's boots and carrying back-packs, gradually at remote stations along the way. Several of these were specially re-opened for the day. While walkers gathered in Leeds, another train sets off from Carlisle, Leeds-bound, and picking up families of Dales folk wishing to spend a day in the city. It all began as an experiment by the Yorkshire Dales National Park with financial help of around £4,000 a year from the Countryside Commission. The above picture shows walkers leaving the Dales Rail service at Appleby railway station in August 1979.

Work begun on the Bramhope tunnel in 1845 and it opened four years later. The tunnel's north portal, seen here, is castellated, and was listed Grade II in 1988. In Otley churchyard there is a monument in the shape of the north portal dedicated to the twenty-four men who lost their lives in the tunnel's construction. The finished tunnel is 2 miles, 243 yards or 2.138 miles (3.441 km) long and 25.5 feet (7.8 m) wide by 25 feet (7.6 m) high. It is a double track tunnel. The construction was for the Leeds Northern Railway and the East & West Yorkshire Junction Railway, which together later became part of the North Eastern Railway.

Goathland, now on the NYMR, was originally known as Goathland Mill. It is on the deviation line opened by the North Eastern Railway in 1865 to avoid the cable-worked Beck Hole Incline, which was part of the original 1836 Whitby & Pickering Railway route. It is seen here in April 1963 when under the threat of closure; villagers argued then that they would be virtually cut off in winter if the railway service was withdrawn.

Grassington & Threshfield station was opened by the Yorkshire Dales Railway on 29 July 1902. The station was situated at the end of an 8.75-mile branch line, the Grassington Branch, which diverged from the Skipton to Ilkley railway at Embsay Junction. At the 1923 'Grouping' the Grassington Branch became part of the LMS, which closed the line to regular passenger services on the 22 September 1930. A caption with the photograph dated 19 April 1949 reads: 'First passenger train in 10 years Leeds to Grassington.' Summer excursions continued to run into the station right up to the 1960s. In August 1969, a final passenger-carrying train ran into Grassington & Threshfield station. The site has since been cleared and developed into a housing estate.

'The end of the line for Exchange Station at Bradford, where the building is disappearing under demolition contractors' bulldozers', reported the *Yorkshire Post* on 28 June 1973. The last train, a special for rail enthusiasts, ran from the station on Saturday 13 January 1973. Trains were then diverted to the city's new bus-rail interchange nearby.

Businessman Brian Taylor, pictured at Clayton West railway station, was featured in the *Yorkshire Evening Post* of 9 August 1989, outlining his plans for a miniature railway at the site. A little later, the Kirklees Light Railway, a 3.5-mile (5.6 km) long, 15-inch (381 mm) gauge, minimum-gauge railway opened in October 1991. It runs along the trackbed of the L&Y's branch line from the village of Clayton West to Clayton West Junction near Shepley on the Penistone Line from Huddersfield to Penistone. The line was originally 1 mile (1.6 km) in length, running from Clayton West station to a specially constructed halt called 'Cuckoo's Nest'. It was extended to Skelmanthorpe in 1992, and again to a station at Shelley in 1997 with a grant from ERDF for the regeneration of coal mining areas. All the locomotives used on the railway were built by the railway's founder, Brian Taylor.

It was goodbye to gas lamps at Cross Gates railway station, Leeds, announced the *Yorkshire Evening Post* in the early 1970s. Electricity was at last taking over. 'Within a stone's throw of the ultra modern Cross Gates centre lies one of the last gas-lit public places in Leeds ... The station illumination dates back to 1902 when the buildings, which have stood there since the station was built in 1834, were modernised and gas lighting was introduced.' Most of the Cross Gates people using the station found the lighting not only a pleasant look back into the past but something they looked forward to seeing in the station at night. Retired Tom Welton said: 'It takes me back to the days when I was just a youngster when I see the comforting glow of the gas lamps as the train pulls into our station.'

In January 1971, the *Yorkshire Post* reported that Tadcaster District Council was demolishing the local railway station and redeveloping the area as an industrial estate. About 2,500 square yards of dressed limestone salvaged from the station buildings was being offered to the Housing Committee. It was to be used in giving an exclusive look to council houses planned for the Hillside area of the town. A £3,375 tender accepted by the council for the demolition and clearance of the buildings included £2,500 for the preparation of the stone.

'Sickened by the continuous din of shunting engines, 66 year old Harold Dawkins decided to sell his grocer's shop near the railway sidings at York ... After viewing 250 houses he found his dream home ... [Nunnington] railway station,' reported the *Yorkshire Evening Post* of 27 August 1959. 'But it was a station almost without trains and mostly derelict. It had not been used by passengers since 1953 and was tumbledown. Harold and his wife, Helen, worked hard repairing the station. They ran a cafe in the waiting room, a small shop in the stationmaster's office and lived comfortably in the adjoining house.'

This Dunford Bridge railway station picture was included in a *Yorkshire Post* feature of 24 August 1971 titled: 'The dying village that hopes to come back with a splash.' It also said that since Dunford Bridge's sudden birth around 1850, when it was the scene of a tunnelling project that forged a rail link between Yorkshire and Lancashire, it has been in turn a railway boom town, a railway village, a border village beauty spot and an army settlement. 'Now the villagers face what could be the final personality change for a plan to construct a £3m reservoir near-by could turn it into a water sports centre,' reported the *Yorkshire Post*.

Members of the Yorkshire Dales Railway Society are seen in December 1969 carrying out a programme of maintenance at Embsay railway station which, at the time, they were hoping to buy and make into their headquarters. From left to right they are Ernest Black, chairman; Graham Hanley; Fred Hunter; and John Brown, events organiser. In subsequent years, the station was re-opened by the Yorkshire Dales Railway (Embsay Railway) on 22 February 1981, having been brought back to its former glory in the days of the LMS. The original Embsay railway station was opened on 1 October 1888 and closed on 22 March 1965.

The official opening of the newly refurbished Fitzwilliam railway station took place in November 1991 amid a row over late trains. Work on the station was carried out as part of a £250, 000 project to improve the Leeds–London line. Children from Kilnsey Middle School helped with bulb planting in the joint venture between Wakefield Council, British Rail and the West Yorks Passenger Transport Executive. But councillors were being urged to ask the WYPTE to press BR to achieve greater standards of time keeping.

BR's property board chairman, Sir James Swaffield, made a brief visit on 16 April 1985 to the dilapidated Halifax railway station. He stressed he was acting in his capacity as a National Civic Trust trustee because he wanted to get a personal view of the town's historic buildings. The station was part of his tour because Calderdale Council wanted to include it in their 'Inheritance Decade' restoration project involving many historic buildings. Sir James and two Trust executives were shown round by two Calderdale planners. Sir James is pictured, right, with planning officer Ernie Grice.

In August 1964, ticket collector David Pexton (left) and John Jefferson, porter, are working on the flower beds at Beverley railway station. Opened in October 1846 by the York & North Midland Railway, Beverley station gained junction status nineteen years later when the NER opened its line to Market Weighton and York. This latter line fell victim to the Beeching Axe on 29 November 1965. The station, which was designed by G. T. Andrews, is now a Grade II listed building and has an elegant overall roof.

The automatic signal box at Tollerton, on the main line north from York, was brought into operation in January 1961. 'Inside the cabin the traditional rows of signal levers have disappeared and instead the signalman sits at a control desk and looks after the passing expresses and goods trains by simply turning a few knobs and switches on a diagram of the track set out in front of him,' reported the *Yorkshire Post*.

Hebden Bridge railway station's current buildings date from 1893, construction having started in 1891. By this time there was a goods yard alongside the station, but this was closed in 1966 and the site is now the station's car park. At the same time, a bus turning circle was constructed and the Booking Office forecourt re-laid and pedestrianised. In 1997, a £1 million renovation project restored the station to its Victorian glory and signage in the original L&Y style was erected. About the same time the Parcels Office was converted into the café. This picture of the station was taken in 1994. (YP Ref 286 94)

Hellifield railway station, pictured in January 1994, before refurbishment.

Hellifield railway station underwent major restoration in 1994/5. Railtrack North East project manager Geoff Bounds is seen in April 1994 with a backdrop of new roof trusses at the station. The restored station was built in 1880 (replacing an earlier, smaller one built in 1849) and soon became a busy junction, as it was located on the MR's main line from London to Scotland. But following the end of regular services in 1962, the line between Blackburn and Hellifeild was used only by special excursion and steam trains or British Rail diversions. Following Hellifield's renovation it returned to commercial use, and trains to and from Carlisle started calling again in May 1995. Between 2005 and 2008, the station was used as the operating base for Kingfisher Railtours' Dalesman steam-hauled charter trains over the Settle–Carlisle Line. The station is also still used by special trains and steam-hauled rail tours as a water stop and traction changeover point.

Horbury and Ossett railway station in 1967 with young train spotters on the platform. The original station was opened in 1840, on the west of the Horbury Bridge Road, to the south-west of the town, but later a new, more substantial structure was built just to the east. Horbury and Ossett station closed in 1970 and Ossett is currently the largest town in Yorkshire without a railway station.

On Monday 13 March 1989, the *Yorkshire Evening Post* reported that work had started on a scheme to clean up Kirkstall Viaduct, which dominated one of the main approaches to Leeds. The twenty-three arches were getting a face-lift as part of a £150,000 scheme jointly funded by British Rail, Leeds Development Corporation and the City Council. Constructed by the Leeds & Thirsk Railway, the viaduct spanning the River Aire and the Leeds–Liverpool canal was designed by Thomas Grainger, using the local Bramley Fall stone, and opened on 23 March 1849. The viaduct is considered by experts to be one of the finest pieces of railway architecture in the region and restoration work was to include re-pointing and the removal of advertising hoardings.

The frontage of Leeds Central station in about 1960. The station closed in 1967, when its services were moved to Leeds City to consolidate all of Leeds' train services in one station.

Pannal railway station's former buildings were extensively extended and converted into a public house in the early 1980s. It was first named Platform One (despite this being located on what is actually now platform 2) but, after another extensive renovation, is currently named The Harwood. When first converted as Platform One, a Pullman kitchen second-class parlour carriage was incorporated into the public house as a dining room. This carriage was removed due to it containing extensive blue asbestos insulation and scrapped by Booths of Rotherham when the public house underwent the second renovation. Originally opened in 1849, Pannal station is operated by Northern Rail, who provide all passenger train services.

When the ceremony to change the name of Staddlethorpe railway station was put off for a month because the nameplates were not ready, children at Gilberdyke Primary School took the opportunity to perfect a song about the occasion. In February 1974, after Councillor Lewis Clayton, chairman of Gilberdyke Parish Council, officially renamed the station, the children stole the scene with their song. The station was renamed to take account of the growth of Gilberdyke as it was felt that Staddlethorpe no longer represented the area the station served.

The picture above illustrated a *Yorkshire Evening Press* article of 3 August 1966 headed 'It's all change at Normanton', which listed some details of the station's past glory: one of the platforms was 500 yards long; around 1870, traffic built up to such a peak that 600,000 passengers and 1,500,000 tons of freight were exchanged in a single year; it was once the Crewe of the coal fields. But by the dawn of the twentieth century, more lines had been opened and fewer and fewer passengers needed to change at Normanton. The article concludes: 'If ever there were to be a station populated with ghosts it would surely be Normanton.'

Oakworth railway station, serving the village of Oakworth, near Keighley, within the City of Bradford Metropolitan District, opened in 1867. It closed in 1962 and was reopened by the K&WVR. The station can still be seen much as it was in the period between 1905 and 1910. It is lit by gas lights, both inside the buildings and on the platform. Milk churns on a hand cart and an old Midland Railway poster bring back images of a former age. The platform fencing is used to display old advertisement signs for products such as Virol. It is famous for being the station in the film *The Railway Children* and was the location for Joe Jackson's music video for 'Breaking Us In Two'. The station is seen here in April 1991.

Archbishop of York, Dr John Sentamu, is at Pickering railway station with Gerry Bacon of the NYMR before a trip to Goathland on 10 October 2006. The Archbishop's visit was part of a timetable that was taking him to each of the twenty-four deaneries in the diocese. Later, Dr Sentamu met staff and volunteers at the historic NYMR as he rode behind a Great Western tank engine pulling a train from Pickering to Goathland. He said: 'The beauty of God's creation is on full display in this deanery. Tourism has really become a substantial business here with a lot of creative thought and energy.'

The dilapidated condition of Pickering railway station since its closure in March 1965 was described in great romantic detail in the *Yorkshire Evening Post* of 13 October 1967 and included the following: 'It was always an embowered halt a regular prize-winner in the annual station gardens competition ... Now three summers after the closure, it's the rosebay willow herbs rather than the roses that hold sway at Pickering. It nods head high in the flower beds and has rooted itself between the tracks ... Most of the station buildings are shuttered and locked and the clock that ticked off the trains on the moorland line stopped at 12.45.' Fortunately, the station was subsequently rescued by the NYMR and returned to its former splendour.

Ravensthorpe station lies on the Huddersfield Line operated by Northern Rail and is 8 miles (13 km) north-east of Huddersfield, just beyond Dewsbury Junction on the former Manchester & Leeds Railway line towards Wakefield Kirkgate and on the main line to Leeds (the former Leeds, Dewsbury & Manchester Railway). It was a late addition to the LNWR line (the station and goods shed were built in 1890, although the line itself opened some forty-two years earlier) to snap up freight work in the area for the company. Currently it is unstaffed, the former station buildings having been demolished after being damaged by fire – seen here – and replaced with basic shelters, and passengers travelling from there must buy their tickets on the train.

Richmond railway station was opened on 9 April 1847 and closed on 3 March 1969. The remaining track was lifted and the building lay derelict until the whole site was acquired by the District Council. Eventually, the passenger terminus became a popular Farm and Garden Centre, although it closed in 2001. In 2003, a community-based project to regenerate Richmond station was given the go-ahead. Work may be seen taking place on an addition to the former railway station in April 2007. The rejuvenated building re-opened – named simply The Station – on 9 November 2007, with two cinema screens, a restaurant and café-bar, an art gallery, a heritage centre, a number of rooms for public use and a range of artisan food-producers.

It was full steam ahead again for the derelict Scholes railway station in August 1979. But the move – costing £100,000 – to put the station back on the rails was not to open the line, but to transform the Victorian station into an attractive public house. And what better name than The Buffers? During April 1979, a thirty-year-old railway dining carriage was brought to the site and carefully lowered on to the rails, into a specially prepared pit alongside the platform. This formed a fifty-two-seat restaurant and created a unique atmosphere. The Hull-based North Country Breweries was behind the idea, which was first given the go ahead in 1977.

Sessay railway station with Class A2 locomotive No. 60533 *Happy Knight* heading the Glasgow–King's Cross passenger train on 13 February 1953. (YP. 5/C683)

In August 1955, stationmaster A. T. Hart (right) and his assistant, Jack Hudson of Cloughton railway station, between Scarborough and Whitby, show an admiring visitor, W. Pickering, a railway motorman, their garden. The garden had won a first-class award every year since 1947, except for 1950, when it took second prize. In 1955, there were over 2,000 plants in the floral scheme. Cloughton railway station opened on 16 July 1885, and closed on 8 March 1965. The station had a canopied goods shed, and in the 1956 *Handbook of Stations* was listed as being able to handle general goods, livestock, horseboxes and prize cattle vans. It also had a 1 ton 10 cwt permanent crane. The station has been restored and is a tearoom, with guest accommodation provided in a converted railway carriage, a converted goods shed and two B&B suites.

David and Karen Hubbard, seen here in February 2007, had converted the old waiting rooms at Hunmanby railway station, near Filey, into a holiday let. The waiting rooms are behind the old station, which is their family home. The station opened for traffic on 20 October 1847 and is currently unstaffed, passengers purchasing their ticket on the train.

Clutching cameras, local people crowded every vantage point at 7.35 a.m. on Saturday 27 March 1982 to get a picture as the 107-year-old brick and stone bridge at Swanhill Lane, Pontefract, was demolished. The man who pressed the button on the detonator to set off more than 650 separate charges was Andrew Hardingham of Sam Contractors Ltd. 'It all went well without any hitches. There was no damage from flying rubble and just two windows were broken by shock waves,' he commented. BR decided that the bridge had to go after it was discovered to have been weakened by subsidence.

On 28 August 1980, the *Yorkshire Post* stated that passengers at Westgate railway station, Wakefield, often admired the rows of colourful flower beds, the hanging baskets and the large display tubs. What they didn't realise was that they were provided free of charge. Gas Board fitter and former professional gardener Ernest Price was such a keen gardener that he provided the station with blooming displays – all for nothing. 'I spend a lot of weekends and evenings up there', said Ernest, who was always being praised for his efforts. 'The passengers like to see the flowers. One American tourist said she had never seen anything like it in the States and took some photographs to show them back home.'

'Sleepy Woodlesford railway station is to be rudely awakened,' reported the *Yorkshire Evening Post* on 13 April 1967. In the period 17–29 April, a number of trains on the Leeds–Knottingley–Goole line and the Sheffield line were to start from Woodlesford for the journey to Goole and terminate at Woodlesford in the reverse direction. Passengers between Leeds and Woodlesford would travel by connecting trains. These arrangements were necessitated by the impending closure of Leeds Central railway station.

York station is deserted on Sunday 29 May 1949 due to a rail strike over the introduction of 'lodging turns'. The following day, the *Yorkshire Post* stated that only two trains ran over the East Coast route; nine excursion trains were cancelled; emergency arrangements were made for travelling post office trains and special services were run in some cases to deliver milk and fish at their destinations; freight services were cancelled and engineering operations including track relaying were postponed.

A rear view, dating from February 1965, of the old York railway station, seen from York city wall. The large Queen Anne-style building beyond the station is the former HQ of the NER. The station was built at the junction of Toft Green, Tanner Row and Station Rise, inside the city walls, by the York & North Midland Railway's architect, George Townsend Andrews, in 1840. It opened on 4 January 1841. Originally a terminus, through-trains calling at York had to reverse out of the station in order to continue their journeys, which was an inconvenience to railway staff and passengers. Consequently, a new through-station (the present York railway station), outside the city walls, was planned and eventually built, opening in 1877. The tracks into the old station, however, remained in use for a further eighty-eight years as carriage storage space. Meanwhile, the railway buildings and hotel were converted into offices.